praise for the freak

D0509085

David Rendall reclaims the term "freak" for what it is — a powerful, game-changing competitive advantage in life and business. This book will change the way you think about being different, and show you how it's the secret to turning around your career.

- **Pam Slim, author of *Escape from Cubicle Nation***

The Freak Factor is an important idea, and David Rendall's is a voice to be reckoned with. We should all look to our lives to see how we can accommodate rather than eliminate the freaks!

- **Nick Morgan, author of *Trust Me: Four Steps to Authenticity* and *Charisma***

Everything you've read about weakness is wrong.... until now. This book will help you stop trying to be well-rounded and start excelling at what you always knew you were best at. Raise your freak flag and wave it with pride!

- **Chris Guillebeau, author of *The Art of Non-Conformity***

Are you a freak? Yes, you are, if you want to be extraordinary. In this provocative book, David Rendall shows why being outstanding comes from first standing out.

~ **Sally Hogshead, author, *FASCINATE: Your 7 Triggers to Persuasion and Captivation***

The FREAK FACTOR

Discovering UNIQUENESS by Flaunting WEAKNESS

David Rendall

We do not believe in ourselves until someone reveals
that deep inside us something is valuable,
worth listening to, worthy of our trust,
sacred to our touch.

— e.e. cummings

Photo of Amber Osborne–bwlphotography.com

Photo of Erika Lyremark–Aaron Sturz

Photo of Jennifer Schuchmann–Paul Daniels

ISBN-13: 978-1456521288
ISBN-10: 1456521284

SEADS Publishing,
Raleigh, North Carolina

To Mrs. Freak and the little freaks

acknowledgements

I want to start by thanking Elliott Anderson. He was the first person who recognized the positive aspects of my seemingly negative characteristics. He is also the first person who called me a freak.

Tom Morris was very influential in the development of this book. He shared countless quotes and articles that supported my idea that weaknesses can be strengths. Because of his deep understanding of the strengths revolution and positive psychology, my friend, Stosh Walsh, was also extremely helpful. My weekly conversations with Joel Rodell have been energizing and my discussions with Allan Bacon have kept me motivated and focused. Mike Lowstetter gave me a copy of *Now, Discover Your Strengths*, which introduced me to an entirely different perspective on personal and career development. Joseph Sherman's consistent correspondence was also invaluable.

Kate Mytty, Jon Mueller and Todd Sattersten at 800-CEO-Read were some of the first people outside of my circle to embrace the freak factor. They supported the creation of the first manifesto and introduced me to many other like-minded people. Sally Hogshead, Pam Slim and Dan Pink have all contributed to this project in a variety of ways. The books of Chris Guillebeau, Parker Palmer, Seth Godin, Ken Robinson and Marcus Buckingham profoundly affected my understanding of life and career success.

I appreciate the many people that have commented on my blog and interacted with me on Twitter and Facebook. Their support for the freak factor message has been tremendously encouraging. Some of them are profiled in the book but I want to also list them here. Matt Langdon, John Wambold, Craig Houston, Bart Gragg, Clemens Rettich, Jeff Brainard, Leah Shapiro, Zane Safrit, Curt Liesveld, Jurgen van Pletsen, Margie Goodchild, Andrew Galasetti, Lance Haun, Chris Ferdinandi, Kate Schreimer, Nellie Felipe, Joe Heuer, Kelly Wall, Jennifer Schuchmann, Sara Dunnigan, Erika Lyremark, Mary Sailors, Amber Osborne, Scott Priestley, Matthew Peters, Roxy Allen, Jean-Philippe Touzeau and Elad Sherf.

Many people that I don't know well have shaped the content of this book by participating in my seminars and classes and responding to my surveys and polls. I have also built some great relationships through my work as a speaker and trainer. Deb Pattison, Susan Barbee, Nick and Nikki Morgan, Don Wells and Esmond Harmsworth have all been instrumental in the success of my business. Eric Smoldt at Group 3 gets all the credit for the design and format of this book and all of my other resources.

My friends and family have also been very supportive, especially, Earl Worley, Bryce Verhaeghe, Mike Ammons, and my mother-in-law, Susan Ford. Finally, this book would not have been possible or meaningful without the love, confidence and assistance of Stephanie, Anna, Emma and Sophia.

outline

foreword

This is a great book about the incredible, outrageous, freakishly wonderful possibility of being exactly who you are–not what someone else may want you to be–and using your amazing distinctiveness to find your own personal form of truly satisfying success.

We all have dreams. But people around us often tell us to "be more realistic." When they give us this advice, what they usually mean is that we should buy into the same assumptions and prejudices about the world that they, and people they know, have absorbed, without sufficient reason. They want us to accept life as they believe it to be, and do more to "fit in." They think that those of us who dream and hope and believe in the rich abundance of new possibility are deluded and disconnected from reality. But it just may be that an atrophy of their own sensibilities has limited their thinking to a shrunken view of reality. Their world may be the emotional size of a postage stamp. But yours need not be at all.

Being properly realistic in our lives and careers doesn't have to mean conforming to the world's most easily available and ready-made patterns, but rather trusting our own innate instincts to guide us into what's right for us as the individuals we are. The greatest advice echoing down the centuries from the ancient world may be the commandment, "Know thyself!" This means knowing not only your passions and joys, along with your obvious strengths, but your weaknesses as well, and considering the possibility that some of those "weaknesses" may really be the keys to hidden strengths that can unlock the doors of astonishing new adventures.

If you go out to a golf course and tee off with a basketball, you can be sure that you won't be getting a hole-in-one. In fact, you'll never sink a single putt. But that's not because there is anything inherently wrong with the basketball. It just deserves a different context where its features are perfect. To see what I mean, try dribbling a golf ball down court on a fast break and taking a three point shot right before the buzzer. You could be using the best golf ball available, but this is clearly the wrong setting for its qualities.

In this book, David Rendall will show you how to be yourself in all your glorious you-ness, and find the right context or setting that fits you like a glove, even if you have to create it yourself–which is often a pretty good idea anyway.

Here's the very good news: You are a freak of nature. There is no one else in the world who can exactly replicate your unique combination of genetics, background, and personal experience. You are one of a kind. There has never been and never will be another you. This book will help you to make the most of this astonishing fact in your life and work.

The ideas here stand in a rich, long tradition, starting perhaps with Socrates, getting reinvented later by Seneca, being refocused along the way by Søren Kierkegaard, and then hitting the shores of America in the work of Ralph Waldo Emerson. Its messages are consistent: Do not cave in to false pressures. Break the artificial chains of the past. Don't conform to the crowd. The ultimate value of aping others can be clearly discerned by a careful consideration of the verb itself. Liberate yourself from average expectations and arbitrary limitations. Be true to yourself. Embrace the glorious freak within. And then bring the world the greatest gift you can give the rest of us–You, in your own elegantly idiosyncratic form of excellence.

This marvelous, fun, and engaging little book will show you how.

Tom Morris, philosopher and author of such books as *True Success*, *The Art of Achievement* and *If Aristotle Ran General Motors*

assessment

Before you start reading, please take a minute to complete this assessment. It will provide you with a clear understanding of your current beliefs about the ideas in this book. If you don't like your score, the rest of the book will show you how to change it.

Respond YES or NO to the following questions. The same assessment appears after the final chapter so you can compare your before and after results.

_____ 1. It is important to fit in at work.

_____ 2. If I want to improve, I need to fix my weaknesses.

_____ 3. I try to build on my strengths, instead of trying to fix my weaknesses.

_____ 4. My job is a good fit for my personality, skills, and interests.

_____ 5. I accept other people's flaws and quirks.

_____ 6. It is important to be well-rounded, especially at work.

_____ 7. I should spend time fixing my weaknesses and building my strengths.

_____ 8. I avoid activities that don't fit my personality, skills, and interests.

_____ 9. Having a well-balanced set of characteristics will make me more marketable.

_____ 10. Being different and sticking out will help me to be more successful in my career.

_____ **Total**

scoring key

1 point each for answering YES to questions 3, 4, 5, 8, 10
1 point each for answering NO to questions 1, 2, 6, 7, 9

Future Freak *(1-2 points)*

You definitely have the potential to become a freak. It seems like you are stuck in situations that don't value your unique characteristics and you're spending a lot of time trying to fix your weaknesses.

Temporary Freak *(3-4 points)*

You're on your way to becoming a freak. It seems like you sometimes build on your strengths but also believe that it is important to fix your weaknesses. You feel like it is important to fit in and be well-rounded at work.

Part-time Freak *(5-6 points)*

You're moving up on the freakness scale. It seems like you're starting to look for situations that make your weaknesses irrelevant and you've begun to see that fixing your weaknesses is an ineffective strategy.

Certified Freak *(7-8 points)*

You are near the top of the freakness scale. You're flaunting your weaknesses most of the time. You avoid most activities that highlight your weaknesses and seek out situations that maximize your strengths.

Superfreak *(9-10 points)*

You are at the pinnacle of freakness. You flaunt your weaknesses and focus on your strengths. You're seeking out the right fit for your unique characteristics and partnering with people that have complementary skills. You also accept other people's freak factor and encourage them to freak out. As a superfreak, are you ready to help others maximize their freak factor?

*This assessment is also available online at freakfactorbook.com/quiz

0. awakening

Everything they told you was wrong

If you come home at the end of the day feeling angry, alienated, and exhausted, maybe you need more than a new job; you need a new line of work.

- Marc Cullen, M.D.

Anna's Symptoms

Anna wakes up at 6am but wishes she could sleep for a few more hours. After getting the kids some breakfast and taking them to school, she drives to the office. Her job pays well and her boss and co-workers are nice enough but she still dreads going to work and at the end of the day she feels so drained, like the life has been sucked out of her.

She's put on a lot of weight over the last few years and she knows that she needs to exercise and eat better but she doesn't have anything left once she gets home. Her lack of energy also makes her impatient and easily irritated, which strains her relationships with her husband and children.

She has read books on time management, stress management, exercise, healthy eating, parenting and marriage but nothing seems to work. Her manager has identified a few areas of improvement on her performance evaluation and has developed an action plan for her to follow. Specifically, she needs to be more flexible and work on her interpersonal skills. She has attended seminars, worked with a coach and tried diligently to achieve the goals in the plan but isn't making much progress.

Anna wants to change. She wants to grow. She's motivated and focused but it just isn't working. She finds herself asking the same questions over and over again.

- What's wrong with me?
- What am I missing?
- Why can't I make any progress?
- What should I do?

If Anna came to you for help, what would you tell her?

- Does she need to try harder?
- Does she need to set clearer goals?
- Does she need therapy?
- Does she need a personal trainer or a life coach?
- Should she join a support group like Weight Watchers?
- Should she get a new job? If so, what kind of job should she look for?

Before we can answer these questions, we need to go back a few years. When Anna was in school, she always got good grades. Although she wasn't the most popular girl in school, she did well in most of her classes and stayed out of trouble. Her teachers consistently commented on her shyness and encouraged her to come out of her shell. School administrators also warned her that she needed to improve her participation and performance in physical education.

Her parents wished that she'd spend less time in her room and more time with other kids and the family. They pushed her to join a sports team or some other extracurricular group activity. Sometimes they'd use terms like anti-social and wondered if she had some kind of disorder. Their fears were just reinforced by Anna's desire to be in control and keep everything very organized. Since she was very little, she'd always been very neat and liked to have things in their proper place. After seeing a special news report on television, her parents even wondered if she might have obsessive-compulsive disorder.

In college, Anna decided to see a counselor after taking an introductory psychology class. Listening to the professor and reading the book convinced her that she wasn't normal and that she needed to get some help. The counselor tried to teach her how to interact more effectively with others and how to be more comfortable with her roommate's messiness. The ideas that Anna learned seemed to make sense but they just didn't stick. She stopped going to her sessions and concluded that she must be lacking in self-discipline or motivation.

For Anna's entire life the people around her, teachers, parents and managers seemed convinced that there was something wrong with her and after a while she started to believe them. How could they all be wrong?

Your Job is Killing You

Anna isn't alone. In talking with my seminar participants, students, friends and family members, I've found a lot of people that are frustrated in their efforts to create the life and career that they've imagined. When I ask students what they want to change about their life, they consistently say that they want to find a better job or start their own business. My experience is supported by a recent Intuit study which showed that 72% of employees "dream of starting their own business" and 67% of respondents said that they "contemplate resigning from their job on a regular basis." Other studies show that 70% of employees are not motivated at work and don't even know how to do their jobs well.

According to a CNN Money report, job satisfaction in the United States hit a 22-year low in 2009. The study found that more than half of American employees are frustrated by their work. "The Conference Board's survey polled 5,000 households, and found that only 45% were satisfied in their jobs. That's down from 61.1% in 1987, the first year the survey was conducted. Even though one in 10 Americans is out of a job, those who are employed are increasingly dissatisfied. 'Through both economic boom and bust during the past two decades, our job satisfaction numbers have shown a consistent downward trend,' said Lynn Franco, director of the Consumer Research Center of The Conference Board.'" The ongoing recession, layoffs, pay cuts and outsourcing promise to make this problem even worse in 2011 and the years to come.

These numbers are staggering! It's not just a few people who are unhappy at work. It is most people. It is the vast majority of people. If you like your job and do it well, you are in the minority. You are rare.

So why am I focusing on work? Why not discuss Anna's other concerns, like health, parenting and marriage? Because I think Anna's poor health, difficult family relationships and lack of sleep are just symptoms of an underlying problem in her career. The root of the problem is work.

As one study showed, problems at work lead to more health issues than financial or family problems. A similar study revealed that 25% believe their job is the biggest source of stress in their lives. This is partly due to the fact that we spend more of our waking hours at work than we spend involved in any other activity. If our job is draining, instead of fulfilling, it will have a dramatically negative impact on our life.

Pam Slim helps people to create alternatives to their current jobs because, in her words, "I found a lot of despair hidden behind smiling faces of smart people in cubicles over the years. Gut wrenching, tears, confusion, sadness, anger, you name it, I heard it." According to Dan Miller, author of *48 Days to the Work You Love*, most suicides occur on Sunday nights and most heart attacks happen on Monday morning. Unfortunately, some people would rather die than go to work and even if they do go to the office, the job kills them anyway.

It is no surprise then that one of the most popular television shows in the United Kingdom and the United States is *The Office*, which chronicles the apathy, incompetence, frustration and futility of corporate life. Similarly, organizations throughout the world are littered with copies of *Dilbert* cartoons, which serve as a comic strip version of *The Office*. Their success shows just how unsuccessful our companies and our employees have become, which is why Pam Slim's book, *Escape from Cubicle Nation* has become a best-seller. The title of the first chapter of the book is a profound question. "I have a fancy title, steady paycheck, and good benefits. Why am I so miserable?"

One of Pam's coaching clients explained it this way. "I describe my office job and cubicle as toxic to my spirit. Before I graduated, I was ambitious, excited and had big dreams. My work sucks all the creativity and fun… and is starting to sap my spirit too. It has dampened my will and motivation and has just made me stop caring. I'm… no longer excited about projects or making a difference. I'm just going through the motions… it's hard to keep the lethargic work energy from spilling over to other aspects of my life."

So why are people so frustrated with their jobs? Why do they want to start their own businesses? People aren't happy in their careers because their job requires them to do work that drains their energy and requires them to be strong where they are weak. A recent Gallup survey found that only 20% of employees feel like they have the opportunity to do what they do best every day. This means that 80% feel trapped by work that relies on them to excel in their areas of weakness. There is a lack of alignment between what we do well and what we have to do at work.

In a Men's Health article, Marc Cullen, M.D., a professor of medicine at Yale University, explains that "the amount of stress you feel from your job has a lot to do with whether the job fits you–that is, whether it matches your personality and style and other demands of your life… If you come home at the end of the day feeling angry, alienated, and exhausted, maybe you need more than a new job; you need a new line of work. The biggest problems are with a misfit. If you're a misfit, fix it–or you'll die trying."

Pam Slim explains that being trapped in the wrong job can lead to:

- Not being able to identify what makes you happy
- A feeling of numbness and emptiness
- A feeling of burning rage
- A feeling of powerlessness and loss of self
- A sense of loneliness
- A loss of direction

Sadly, no one seems that interested in helping people to find the right fit. In fact, well-meaning parents, schools, employers and psychologists systematically teach people how to fit in, instead of showing them how to match their talents and passions to their activities.

What is Your Biggest Weakness?

While researching ideas for the book, I did a Google search for "strengths and weaknesses." The majority of the results were instructions on how to properly answer the interview question, "What is one of your weaknesses?" It is worth noting that this is one of the most common questions asked by interviewers.

The advice that I found varies, but falls into three basic categories. First, tell them about a weakness that you have already improved and explain your plan for continued improvement. For example, you could explain that you struggle with new technology, but have started playing a lot of online video games to help you get more comfortable with computers and the internet.

Second, discuss a weakness that is unrelated to the job. For example, in an interview for a job as construction worker, you could admit to having poor computer skills or body odor or a habit of yelling inappropriate comments at attractive women. Third, focus on a weakness that has an upside for the company. For example, you can confess that you work too hard and are so committed to the company that you don't ever take time to relax. Describing yourself as a suck-up or major brown-noser might also be helpful.

All of this advice seems to assume that you have something to hide from the interviewer and that you are trying to keep them from discovering who you really are. If you are successful, then you'll be rewarded with a job and a boss that assumes you don't have any relevant weaknesses or that you are willing and able to fix any of your weaknesses. As Seth Godin explains in *Linchpin,* "If you need to conceal your true nature to get in the door, understand that you'll probably have to conceal your true nature to keep that job."

Is that the kind of job that you want? Is that the way to find the right fit? Well, it doesn't really matter because, if you need a job, those are the answers that employers are looking for.

Once you have the job, most managers keep asking the question about your biggest weakness on an annual or semi-annual basis. It's called the performance evaluation. This is because most companies require that evaluations focus on performance issues or developmental challenges or areas for improvement. All of these are terms to describe weaknesses.

Organizations are requiring their managers to find and document weaknesses and create plans for fixing them in the appraisal process. In fact, this is usually seen as the primary purpose of the appraisal. The positive aspects of the employee's performance are quickly reviewed or acknowledged and then the majority of the time is spent on repairing flaws.

We know that employees dread their performance review but did you know that managers feel the same way? Evaluations are one of the tasks that supervisors like the least. This

The Freak Factor

is probably because they are so negative and, after doing them for years, most managers understand that doing the appraisal this way doesn't actually improve anyone's performance. This is why a lot of supervisors only complete the review process as a formality that is required by the human resources department.

To make matters worse, many companies now use 360-degree feedback tools that allow everyone to participate in the evaluation process. Instead of only being put down by your boss, you can now get criticism from your boss, peers and subordinates.

Freak Profile: Nellie Felipe

The ineffectiveness of the conventional approach to improvement at work is illustrated by Nellie's experience during one of her performance evaluations. I met Nellie, founder of Arize Coaching and Consulting, at a seminar for entrepreneurs and she shared the following story with me. You can find out more about Nellie at arizecc.com.

"One incident in particular, midway through my career, stands out. Though the years have flown by, I still remember it as if it were yesterday.

I was in my manager's office going over my annual review. I was so excited. My 360-degree feedback was excellent. On a scale of 1 to 5, I was rated 4.7. As a Senior Project Manager that was an awesome achievement. Project Managers assign people more work to their already full plate along with a tight deadline and then chase them for a status updates. So, naturally, project managers are not the most popular people in the company.

My manager and I began walking through the annual review section by section. I was elated, that is until we got to the Interpersonal Skills section. I was in shock to see that I had only been given 3 out of 5. I believe that I am the ultimate people-person.

Without looking up at me, my manager tactfully went on to ask me to stop smiling and acting enthusiastic while I was at work. OUCH! My mind screamed 'please pinch yourself and pray that you are having a nightmare.' This could not be happening. Job descriptions frequently read 'enthusiastic, results-oriented professional with…'

My manager explained that he thought I was fantastic and his best, most productive and dependable employee. However, one of the senior executives was annoyed by my natural enthusiasm. My boss asked me to stop smiling at this executive when I passed her in the hallways. 'You can acknowledge her. Just do not smile.'

Wow! This pierced my being. I was born enthusiastic, smiling and looking at the brighter side of everything. His quote from her was 'if people want sunshine they could go outside.' The fact that I had delivered 180% of my set goals went by the wayside."

Nellie's story has a happy ending but her eventual success was not facilitated by her manager or her organization. She succeeded because she refused to accept this ridiculous criticism and change her approach to work.

"I have a love and passion for life and people. I knew immediately that I could not change this about me because it is deeply ingrained. Fast forward to today. I run a business and am a successful business consultant, change manager, and coach; all of which requires that a person be enthusiastic, encouraging, and genuinely caring. I am so glad that my enthusiasm was not easily turned off; otherwise this high-level executive, who I highly respected, would have killed the precise trait that propels me."

This manager was doing his best to improve the Nellie's performance. He thought that, by pointing out her flaws and asking her to change, he would get the desired result. However, he almost inadvertently killed the traits that propelled her.

This approach is all too common but it would be wrong to focus exclusively on the workplace. Managers and employees are just doing what they've been taught by parents, teachers and psychologists. In other words, the problems at work start with the incorrect beliefs that we learn at home and school. The people who should be forming us are often guilty of deforming us.

The Freak Factor

We are all apt to believe what the world believes about us.

- George Eliot

Deforming Beliefs

There are four beliefs that contribute to our feelings of stress and frustration in our careers. First, we believe that to be successful, we need to be normal, to fit in and not stand out. This means that we should follow the rules and do what we're told. Second, we think that we should be flexible, balanced and well-rounded by fixing weaknesses and improving our flaws. Third, we're convinced that we could fit in, if we just tried hard enough. Finally, we could fix our weaknesses, if we just had enough self-discipline and perseverance.

All of these beliefs seem empowering but they are actually debilitating. They tell us that we have the potential to succeed, that we have the ability, but they misguide us as to where that potential lies and how we should apply that potential. They set us up for failure and then lead to confusion and disappointment when we don't achieve our goals. This creates a downward spiral as we keep relying on the same incorrect beliefs and ineffective actions to correct the very problem that these myths created in the first place.

Unfortunately, the people who should be teaching us how to succeed in our lives and careers are the very people who teach and reinforce these myths. As Parker Palmer explains in *Let Your Life Speak,* "We arrive into this world with birthright gifts–then we spend the first half of our lives abandoning them or letting others disabuse us of them. As young people, we are surrounded by expectations that may have little to do with who we really are, expectations held by people who are not trying to discern our selfhood but to fit us into slots. In families, schools, workplaces, and religious communities, we are trained away from true self toward images of acceptability; under social pressures... our original shape is deformed beyond recognition; and we ourselves, driven by fear, too often betray true self to gain the approval of others."

Recovering From Our Education

Schools add to the problem by teaching children that they need to be balanced and well-rounded individuals who excel equally in all areas. If you get an A in English but a failing grade in Math, you don't move to the next grade. If you can't demonstrate reasonable competence across a variety of subjects on a standardized test, you won't move ahead or you'll be denied admission to college. If you love science but hate gym, you'll be continually pushed to work on your physical fitness, usually by an overweight gym teacher.

If you ask about the practical value of subjects like algebra, you'll get vague answers about critical thinking or reasoning skills or an admission that algebra is just a requirement so you need to study in order to graduate. The lesson of school is clear. Effective people are knowledgeable in all areas of life and do equally well across the entire spectrum of academic subjects. Students who fight against this belief system are criticized, disciplined, medicated, suspended and expelled.

In his book, *The Element*, Sir Ken Robinson argues for a complete transformation of the educational system in most industrial nations because of the way our schools destroy the potential of so many students. "I believe passionately that we are all born with tremendous natural capacities, and that we lose touch with many of them as we spend more time in the world. Ironically, one of the main reasons this happens is education. The result is that too many people never connect with their true talents and therefore don't know what they're really capable of achieving. In that sense, they don't know who they really are."

Robinson says that "some of the most brilliant, creative people I know did not do well at school. Many of them didn't really discover what they could do–and who they really were–until they'd left school and recovered from their education." And he offers numerous examples throughout the book, including Virgin founder and billionaire, Richard Branson.

He specifically criticizes the way that schools teach children to be normal. "Public education puts relentless pressures on its students to conform… The current processes of education do not take account of individual learning styles and talents. In that way, they offend the principle of distinctiveness."

I experienced this pressure to conform throughout my years in school. I wasn't very popular with my teachers in school. One particular English teacher had a special distaste for me. She might have disliked me because I wrote a creative writing paper on the subject of vomit, for which I received a grade of F. I was under the mistaken impression that when she said we could write about anything, that she actually meant it. To be honest, I probably knew that she didn't mean it, but maybe I wanted her to acknowledge that she didn't actually want us to be creative.

On another similar assignment, I wrote the entire paper using as many B words as I could think of. Every possible word started with the letter B, except for the occasional "and" or "the." Again, this was fairly creative from my perspective. Unfortunately, my teacher wasn't as impressed and wasn't as generous with the Bs. The paper got me another F.

I didn't think much of it at the time. I knew that I wouldn't get a good grade and I can't really argue that I had some higher purpose in writing the paper. It wasn't a political statement and I wasn't an artistic genius… or was I?

The Freak Factor

Many years later I was sitting on the couch with my two daughters reading stories to them before bedtime and I picked up *The Berenstain's B* Book. It was an entire children's book based on the same principle as my school paper. Use as many Bs as you can in one book so that kids learn the letter and the associated words. The story is ridiculous but it doesn't matter. That isn't the point. The point is to teach the letter B to kids.

The book culminates in the lines "Big brown bear, blue bull, beautiful baboon blowing bubbles biking backward, bump black bug's banana boxes and Billy Bunny's breadbasket and Brother Bob's baseball bus and Buster Beagle's banjo-bagpipe-bugle band and that's what broke Baby Bird's balloon."

Someone got paid to write a story just like the one that earned me a failing grade. The fact that someone published a book with Random House doing exactly what I did seems important. My teacher did what most people do. When they see something that is different, they reject it. She wanted me to be normal. She wanted me to do things right. She wanted me to see that I had a problem following instructions or being a good student. But she missed the bigger issue.

I was being creative. It may have looked like immaturity or silliness, but it could have been redirected. She could have recognized and encouraged the potential. It does take a certain amount of imagination and vocabulary to be able to write an entire paper without using any words that don't start with B.

What would have happened if my teacher would have given me an A and told me that I was an amazingly inventive soul? What if she would have encouraged me to use my talents to become a writer? What if she would have told me that I could use my off-beat sense of humor to become successful? I can't answer those questions because it didn't happen and it took me years to recover from my education.

But maybe we should excuse our schools because they are just trying to prepare students for a career in an organizational environment that is very similar to school. In his book, *Linchpin,* Seth Godin explains that our schools were designed more than a century ago to train people for factory work and they continue to prepare students to toil in our modern cubicle factories. Factories thrive on standardization and mass production, not individuation and customization. When students struggle with this artificial and restrictive environment, we diagnose them with psychological disorders and give them medication to help them behave, to fit in, to act normal.

Paulo's Parents

Our parents have a powerful influence on our lives and careers. However, this influence can often be quite negative. In *The Element* Ken Robinson tells the story of Paulo Coelho, a young man who wanted to be a writer. Unfortunately, his parents thought that Paulo should be a lawyer and that writing was nothing more than a hobby. When Paulo resisted their advice and pursued his writing career, his parents had him committed to a psychiatric institution where he was given electroshock treatments. His parents did this because they loved him and wanted what was best for him. But their notions of what was best included having a normal life with a good job doing respectable work that paid a good salary.

You might be thinking that this is an extreme case, that most parents don't go this far to force their children to follow a path that doesn't match their interests or abilities. Sometimes their resistance is subtle, like in the ways parents criticize children for their annoying habits. It can be difficult for children to identify pursue their unique talents and goals without the guidance and support of their parents. It is even harder when their parents actively resist that pursuit.

Adam's parents remember that he was always screaming as a child. Adam explains, "Apparently, I was a real pain in the butt in restaurants. They couldn't take me anywhere. I was super super noisy… I was very talkative, very hyperactive. I was bouncing off the walls all the time. Not much different than I am now really." He was noisy, so they told him to be quiet. They didn't take him out because it was embarrassing to have a child who wasn't normal and quiet and obedient.

Adam has grown up but he's still screaming and noisy and now he has a full band and sound system to accompany him and amplify his voice. Although his parents used to tell him to be quiet, I bet they're happy that he didn't listen. Because he was the runner-up on *American Idol* in 2009 and his first album sold nearly a million copies worldwide, more than Kris Allen, the 2009 winner.

When I was a kid, my parents nicknamed me "motor-mouth" because my mouth never stopped running. I was always hungry and at the leftovers from everyone else's plate at restaurants, so they called me "the vulture."

Once I brought home a report card from school. I got an A in every subject, except English. There, I was getting a C. How did my parents respond? Did they compliment me on my excellent work in most of my classes? Did they encourage me to focus my efforts on those areas where I was having success? No. Instead, they wanted to talk about English. What was I doing wrong? How could I do better? Was I trying hard enough?

They believed, as most parents do, that we all need to be well-rounded. But before we put too much of the blame on parents, let's remember that they teach kids to be normal and well-rounded because they want their kids to succeed in the workplace. That is what companies seem to want, average and obedient employees.

The scrutiny doesn't end when you leave home. As an adult, your spouse and children also have strong feelings about what you should and shouldn't do with your life and career. They might not care as much about your personal fulfillment as they do about their financial security or material well-being. The people who are closest to us are also the most likely to uncover and address our deepest flaws. We might be able to hide some weaknesses from others but our families tend to know us better than anyone else.

Negative Psychology

The roots of all of these myths and counterproductive behaviors can be found in the study and practice of psychology. For more than 100 years, psychologists have been creating, diagnosing and treating our mental disorders. Based on the medical model of identifying and repairing illness, psychology has a negative focus. Counselors and psychiatrists are trained to find and fix our weaknesses. They don't study mental health. They study mental illness. They don't study happiness. They study depression. They don't diagnose satisfaction and fulfillment. They diagnose disappointment and pain.

This approach to psychology might not be so bad if it was actually working. The past 100 years of medicine have virtually eliminated some diseases, like polio, discovered preventative measures and treatments for many other previously deadly conditions and produced a tremendous increase in lifespan and quality of life. In other words, medical science has helped us to become healthier.

Psychology can't claim the same success. No cures for mental illness have been discovered in the history of psychology. There has been no decrease in mental illness and no rise in mental health. In fact, it is quite the opposite. If anything, psychology has produced a dramatic increase in the number of people who would identify themselves as depressed, neurotic, anxious and obsessive compulsive. For many people, therapy has become a basic life activity, just like going to the gym or doing some shopping.

The default assumption is that there is probably something wrong with all of us and it probably wouldn't hurt to talk to a counselor about it. But I think it probably does hurt. Talking to a counselor just reinforces our belief that we are different and that we should work harder to be more normal. It also encourages us to focus time, energy and effort on discovering and deleting our liabilities.

In general, I think psychologists over-diagnose and over-medicate mental illness. In other words, they convince us that something is wrong, when there's nothing wrong and then they give us a pill to fix our supposed sickness. The only guarantee is that the side effects of the medication will probably be worse than our original symptoms. The overall effect is that we have become a society that is dominated by the negative psychological paradigm and we no longer think to challenge the assumptions of this view, even though it has failed to help us live better lives.

Self-Destruction Books

The self-improvement book and seminar business has a track record that is similar to that of psychology. The whole industry is built on telling you what is wrong with you, getting you to feel guilty about your shortcomings and then selling you a solution to your problems. Again, it seems like a very empowering thing to do. But given the dramatic increase in the number and availability of self-help resources, why don't we see an equal increase in people's performance?

Why do most of the self-help books in the 21st Century offer the same advice as those written in the 20th Century? Why do self-help books in the 21st Century try to help us fix the same problems that people had in the 20th Century? Why haven't we made any progress?

We haven't made any progress because self-improvement is premised on the same foundations as psychology. Are you disorganized? Read a book on how to be more organized. Are you too shy? Go to a seminar on how to be more outgoing. Are you a pushover? Take a class on how to be more assertive. What could be simpler? But if it is so simple, then why are so many of us still struggling?

The fact is that millions of messy people read books on how to be more organized and try to apply what they've learned but they just can't. Millions of shy people attend seminars on how to be more outgoing and try to implement what they've been taught but they just can't. Millions of non-confrontational people take classes on how to be assertive and try to stand up to others but they just can't. What's their problem? Why can't they change? Why isn't self-help helping? Is it possible that self-improvement is actually self-destructive?

One Question

As a college professor, I teach classes in personal effectiveness, strategic planning and managing change. I try to help people improve their personal lives and their organizations. Over the years, I've asked a lot of students to explain why they failed to make important changes in their lives or failed to achieve their goals. One of the common answers is a lack of self control. Person after person describes a sincere desire to improve, but is unable to carry it out. The goal of the class is to help them overcome the barriers to successful planning and change.

Throughout this process, I try to teach people how to change and how to plan. For example, most strategic planning starts with a SWOT analysis, which is an exploration of the organization's Strengths, Weaknesses, Opportunities and Threats. Similarly, most guides to self-improvement stress the importance of self-awareness. We need an honest and relatively complete understanding of ourselves in order to grow and succeed.

However, I've found little guidance to help people understand what to change and what to plan. What should people do with their self-awareness? What kinds of things should we try to change? What if there are some things we can't change or shouldn't change? Specifically, when confronted with our strengths and weaknesses how should we respond?

I believe strongly in our ability to learn and grow. However, I've watched so many people struggle with change that I'm not convinced we can change anything we want to. I'm not convinced that we need, or can find, more self control or willpower. Maybe we're trying to change the wrong things. Maybe we're setting the wrong goals.

These questions have led me to focus more on teaching students what to change, what to plan and what to do with their awareness of strengths and weaknesses. I start by asking a simple multiple-choice question.

If you want to increase your personal and professional effectiveness, should you:

1. Fix your weaknesses
2. Build on your strengths
3. Do both (fix your weaknesses and build on your strengths)

The overwhelming majority of students choose option three, both fix weaknesses and build on strengths. In many situations, no one will choose to just build on their strengths, but someone will always choose to just fix weaknesses. This result is consistent with research by the Gallup Organization which indicates that 59% of respondents believed that fixing weaknesses was essential to personal development. Only 41% chose building strengths as the path to success.

In the Gallup study "doing both" wasn't offered as an option. However, I suspect that offering people the option of doing both would have drastically decreased the number of those that chose to build on their strengths.

I follow up by asking students to support their choice. Why did they choose their answer? It is interesting to explore their rationale for each answer.

Those that chose to fix their weaknesses gave the following reasons:

- I'll turn my weaknesses into strengths and then I'll be even stronger.
- You don't need to build on strengths because they will always be there. They are natural. You don't have to maintain them.
- Nobody is perfect. There is always room for improvement.

- You are only as strong as your weakest link.

- I can think of more weaknesses than strengths.

- Weaknesses make you look bad. Managers, co-workers and others notice your weaknesses and use them against you.

Those that choose to both fix weaknesses and build strengths offer similar reasons.

- It is important to be well-rounded and balanced.

- You can't ignore your weaknesses because they will trip you up.

- It is easier to be balanced than great. It is hard to be so good that your weaknesses are irrelevant.

- You should work on as many things as you can.

- There is always room for improvement.

Those that choose to build on strengths believe that:

- You can't be good at everything.

- There is a place for everyone.

- Nobody is perfect. You'll always have weaknesses so don't worry about them.

- Our weaknesses make us human.

- It is important to see the best in people and bring out the best in others.

- Strengths make up for our weaknesses. A great offense makes up for a bad defense.

- It is more enjoyable to build on strengths.

- Strengths are where you have the greatest chance of becoming exceptional.

As you can see, there are many different reasons supporting each approach. The validity of these beliefs and the effectiveness of each will be explored throughout the rest of the book. For now, it is enough to note that the beliefs that support fixing weaknesses and doing both are significantly different from the beliefs that support building on strengths.

It might be helpful at this point to note the responses that fit best with your current belief system. How would you respond to the one question quiz? Why?

The Freak Factor Survey

I wanted to get a better sense of people's beliefs about strengths, weaknesses and career development, so I created my own survey, which has been completed by hundreds of people throughout the world over the last year. The survey is nearly identical to the self-assessment at the beginning of this chapter.

The survey results confirmed my experience in the classroom. Overall, 48% of respondents believed that they need to fit in, fix weaknesses and be well-rounded in order to succeed in their careers.

- 50% agreed and only 35% disagreed with "It is important to fit in at work." *

- 52% agreed and only 35% disagreed with "If I want to improve, I need to fix my weaknesses."

- 52% agreed and only 33% disagreed with "It is important to be well-rounded, especially at work."

- 52% agreed and only 30% disagreed with "I should fix my weaknesses and build my strengths."

- 56% agreed and only 26% disagreed with "A well-balanced set of characteristics will make me more marketable."

- Nearly 25% responded "not sure" to "Being different and sticking out will help me in my career."

*agree/disagree percentages don't equal 100 because some respondents chose "not sure."

The results of this survey are important because our beliefs have a profound influence on our actions. Furthermore, the validity of those beliefs has a major influence on the effectiveness of our actions. If we believe the wrong things then our actions will be ineffective and self-defeating. If we believe the right things, then our actions have the potential to be fruitful and fulfilling. The power of our beliefs is illustrated painfully and beautifully by the story of an elementary school teacher in Iowa.

What Color are Your Eyes?

In April 1968, Jane Elliott taught her third-grade students an important lesson. She divided the class into two groups based on eye color. The children were then told that blue-eyed children were smarter, kinder and cleaner than brown-eyed children. Because of this blue-eyed children were given extra privileges in the classroom. For example, they were allowed to be first in line and got a longer recess.

Brown-eyed children had to wear special collars that designated them as inferior and their actions were consistently criticized by Elliott throughout the day. As the day progressed, the supposedly superior blue-eyed children began to tease and insult those with the inferior eye-color. Because of this treatment, the inferior children became withdrawn and sad. They also decreased participation in class activities. In discussions with Elliott, they admitted that they were indeed less intelligent than their blue-eyed classmates and their test results and other schoolwork for the day showed a marked decrease in performance.

0. awakening

The next day, Elliott explained to the students that she had made a mistake. The brown-eyed children were actually superior to the blue-eyed ones. The response to this announcement was immediate and profound. The brown-eyed children began to celebrate, while the blue-eyed children became despondent. As with the day before, the newly superior brown-eyed children began to criticize their supposedly inferior counterparts. The inferior children showed a significant decrease in confidence, energy and effort, while the apparently superior students demonstrated a commensurate increase in positive attitude, engaged activity and overall success.

Elliott used this exercise to teach her students about discrimination. It was the day after the assassination of Martin Luther King Jr. and her students in Riceville, Iowa lived in an all-white community of just under 1,000 people. She wanted to help them understand the insidious nature of prejudice and stereotypes. She did this when she chose "a physical characteristic over which they had no control and attributed negative elements to this characteristic."

It is obvious to external observers, especially adults, that there is no real advantage to having a particular eye color. The apparent superiority of the blue-eyed or brown-eyed students was just an illusion. It wasn't real. It was just an exercise. However, the belief that one eye-color was good and the other was bad had a major impact on students' behaviors and performance.

This exercise illustrates the power of our thoughts in determining how we act. More importantly, it illustrates the incredible change that takes place when we discover that what we thought was bad is actually good, that what we thought was a weakness is actually a strength. Imagine the response of the brown-eyed students when, after a day of humiliation and criticism, the teacher announced that they weren't inferior. Imagine their joy and excitement. Imagine their transformation.

What if the same was true for you? What if what you thought was bad turned out to be good instead? What if your apparent weaknesses were just an illusion? What if the people that have been criticizing you were wrong? What your teachers, bosses, co-workers and spouse had made a mistake? How would you feel? What would you do?

I think we all experience some form of Elliott's exercise every day. There are three stages to this process. First, other people take a characteristic over which we have "no control" and "attribute negative elements to it." Second, we believe that the criticism is true. We listen to their charges and take them to heart. Third, we feel bad. We wish we could change. We vow to turn things around. We promise to do better but we can't. Gradually, as it did with Elliott's students, the frustration begins to erode our happiness and reduce our performance.

It doesn't have to be this way. The truth is that your critics are wrong and your weaknesses are just an illusion.

It's never too late to be who you might have been.

— George Eliot

New Beliefs

So far we've discussed two lies that lead to frustration and failure in our lives and careers. The first lie is that being normal, following the rules and fitting in will help you to succeed. The second lie is that fixing your weaknesses, being balanced and well-rounded is the best route to personal and career fulfillment.

I just found out there's no such thing as the real world,
just a lie you've got to rise above.

- John Mayer, *No Such Thing*

We need to replace these self-defeating beliefs with two more accurate and useful assumptions. First, it is good to be different, to stick out and to be a freak. Second, it is good to flaunt your weaknesses, instead of fixing them. It is good to be unbalanced.

Conformity is the ruin of the mind.

- Jesse Shelley

Most People

Chris Guillebeau's book, *The Art of Non-Conformity*, argues that "you don't have to live your life the way other people expect you to. You can do good things for yourself and make the world a better place at the same time." Unfortunately, most of us adjust our behavior based on what most people do. This seems to be human nature. Psychologists refer to it as social proof. We figure that if most people are doing something, then it must be a good idea. Unfortunately, this isn't true.

- Most people are employees
- Most people don't like their work
- Most people only have a high school education
- Most people are in debt
- Most people make less than $50,000 per year

- Most people don't exercise regularly
- Most people think they'll succeed by fixing their weaknesses

- A select few start their own businesses
- A select few do what they love
- A select few graduate from college
- A select few are debt free
- A select few earn a six-figure income
- A select few exercise regularly
- A select few flaunt their weaknesses, instead of trying to fix them

I'm not arguing that starting a business, having a college degree or earning a lot of money are the most important things in life. My point is that you probably don't want what most people have. You probably want what only a select few have. But if you do what most people do, if you follow the crowd, then you probably won't have the life that you want. Non-conformity is important because you probably want to be like a select few, instead of ending up like most people.

I'm not going to change the way I look or the way I feel to conform to anything. I've always been a freak.

— John Lennon

Differentiation

After a speaking engagement in Boston, I was doing some shopping and saw this sign for sale in a small store. It read "I think the only normal people are the ones you don't know too well." This is important. There is no such thing as normal. We only imagine that other people are normal. Similarly, other people know they aren't normal, but assume that we are.

Even if it was good to be normal, it isn't possible. No one is normal. It is just an abstract concept that doesn't exist in reality.

A lot of people pay lip service to the value of being different. An essential marketing strategy for most organizations includes achieving significant differentiation from their competition. However, it is difficult to be different. When others notice that you are different, they try to make you fit in.

Robert Quinn argues in *Deep Change* that "deviance will always generate external pressures to conform… If you perform beyond the norms, the systems will adjust and try to make you normal." Einstein put it more strongly when he said, "great spirits have always experienced violent opposition from mediocre minds."

Matt Langdon at *The Hero Construction Company* teaches kids that they can be heroes in everyday situations. One of Matt's posts about the movie *The Tale of Despereaux* argues that it is good to be strange. The post begins with a quote from the movie, which is a cartoon about a mouse with extraordinarily large ears and tremendous courage.

"'Reader, you must know that an interesting fate awaits almost everyone, mouse or man, who does not conform.' When you act heroically, you're going to stand out. Despereaux's ears were not the only thing that made people notice him. His courage, thoughts of a better world, and kindness made him stand out. They also made him the object of disdain and mockery. Heroes are ordinary people who do extraordinary things, so there will always be a majority to think the hero's behavior is wrong, dangerous, or weird. Heroes don't cower and they don't subscribe to the ideas of the masses just because those ideas are popular."

Some will always see deviance as wrong and dangerous, so they respond with disdain and mockery. That is why E. E. Cummings warned "It takes courage to grow up and turn out to be who you really are." It can be risky to stick out. Because of this, we tend give up on being who we really are and instead we just do what other people are doing.

We want to fit in. We don't want to be different or unusual. We don't want to stick out. It seems safe to be normal. Why risk "violent opposition?"

However, it can be just as dangerous to simply remain average. Management guru, Tom Peters argues that "The White Collar Revolution will wipe out indistinct workers and reward the daylights out of those with True Distinction." He believes that it is no longer safe to be the same, to be normal, to be indistinct. Let that sink in for a minute. He is saying that the only safe move, the only prudent choice, the only wise decision is to become a freak, to be unusual, different, strange and remarkable.

Fitting in is a short term strategy.
Standing out pays off in the long run.

- Seth Godin

Dumb or Different?

Don Wells, a wonderful friend and consultant, sent me this story about a student who seemed dumb, but he wasn't. He was just different. "When I was head of the middle school at the Friends School, there was a 14 year old, Tommy, who was severely dyslexic. I ran a six week course about perception with about 15 students in it. One day I said that we were going for a stroll about the school grounds and when we returned I would ask them 20 questions about things that we would see on our walk. For example, were there any red cars in the parking lot? They could take any notes that they wanted to, and the things that I would ask would not be trick questions.

We walked and everyone took notes and looked earnestly, except Tommy. He just strolled along and observed. That was it. When we got back to the classroom, I gave everyone a piece of paper with 20 questions on it. There were some very smart kids in the classroom and it was well known that Tommy struggled in almost every class.

Kids finished and exchanged papers and then we went down the answers. The highest score out of 20 seemed to be 14, by perhaps the smartest kid in the class. However, Tommy got 18 out of 20! The class and I were stunned. They asked 'how do you do it?' Tommy, a bit embarrassed, simply said 'I just looked.'

Students were not convinced, so they persuaded me, and Tommy, to do it again in the next class. We did and got the same results as he blew everyone else away, even though kids were watching him for any clues.

His Mom and Tommy struggled greatly about the stigma of his performance in school. But from that day on Tommy was never dismissed as dumb. He simply viewed things with a different eye than others and it worked. His Mom, a few days afterward, came into my office and hugged me while sobbing saying that Tommy's life changed that day. What a gift! Tommy went on to graduate from North Carolina State with a degree in design and has a successful business near Memphis."

The Freak Factor

That which has always been accepted by everyone,
everywhere, is almost certain to be false.

- Paul Valery

As a young man, Albert Einstein was also criticized by most of his teachers and was considered a "dullard" because of his independent and unconventional approach to life and learning. He went on to become one of the most admired and influential scientists in history by attacking the foundational assumptions of math and science. Einstein's enduring greatness supports Seth Godin's assertion that "if you want to get better than conventional results, it's important to ignore the conventional wisdom."

Einstein and Tommy are not isolated cases. It seems that success absolutely requires you to be different. In his book, *Deep Change,* management professor, Robert Quinn, explains that "Excellence is a form of deviance… The way to achieve and maintain excellence is to deviate from the norm. You become excellent because you are doing things that normal people do not want to do."

Nerds are a good example of the relationship between excellence and deviance. The very habits that make these people so awkward and disliked in school are the very traits that often lead to their incredible success. This is why Microsoft founder, Bill Gates, once quipped, "Be nice to nerds. Chances are you'll end up working for one."

When my middle daughter started kindergarten, they assigned each child to a reading group based on their ability. But when I asked her who was in her group, she said that she was the only one. The teacher seemed to be confused about the definition of the word "group," so I went to talk with her. She explained that my daughter's reading ability was so much better than the other students' that she didn't have anyone else to put in the group. My daughter didn't fit in because she wasn't normal, but this wasn't because she was bad, it was because she was good, because she was better.

Read, every day, something no one else is reading…
It is bad for the mind to be always part of unanimity.

- **Christopher Morley**

It might be hard to base your differentiation efforts on the fact that my six-year old is a good reader. That is understandable. So let's take a look at Warren Buffet, one of the richest and most generous people in the world. He explained his formula for success in a New York Times article, written during the spectacular meltdown of the financial sector in 2008. "Be fearful when others are greedy, and be greedy when others are fearful." In other words, his formula for success is to do the opposite of what everyone else is doing. He's different. He's a deviant.

Michael Lewis wrote *The Big Short* to tell the story of the few people who predicted and prepared for the crash of the sub-prime mortgage industry. One of the people he profiled was Mike Burry, a neurologist in California who has Asperger's syndrome, a form of autism. Burry's investment company, Scion Capital, had returns of 490% from 2000 to 2008, when the Standard and Poor's 500 returned only 2% during that same period.

Burry saw the demise of the real estate sector as early as 2005 and made nearly a billion dollars when it imploded. When asked to explain his special insight and willingness to go against the grain, he credited his success to the example of Warren Buffet. Burry believes that Buffet's life proves that "to succeed in a spectacular fashion you have to be spectacularly unusual." Many of us miss out on spectacular success because we are unwilling to be spectacularly unusual.

How does Jim Cramer, the manic host of *Mad Money*, explain his success? In an interview for Esquire he said, "I'm a freak of nature. I'm just a freak. I'm just a freak." He's not lying and he's not exaggerating. He is definitely not normal. Cramer's success and his strangeness prove that it is indeed good to be a freak.

The Freak Factor

Don't try to stand out from the crowd. Avoid crowds altogether.

- Hugh MacLeod, *Gaping Void*

Seven Reasons to be Different

1. Being different makes you **rare**. Being normal makes you **ordinary**.

    Scarcity increases value. Diamonds are valuable primarily because they are rare. Sand and salt are far less valuable, not because they aren't useful, but because they are so ordinary and plentiful.

I'm the boss. I don't make copies. I make originals.

- Michael Scott, *The Office*

2. Being different makes you **original**. Being normal makes you easy to **imitate**.

    One reason that many jobs are outsourced or computerized is that they've become so routine that they are easy to automate and simple for others to learn and duplicate. Keith Ferrazzi, in his book *Never Eat Alone*, argues that we must "be distinct or be extinct… The best brands, like the most interesting people, have a distinct message… When it comes to making an impression, differentiation is the name of the game. Confound expectation. Shake it up. How? There's one guaranteed way to stand out in the professional world. Be yourself."

    Similarly, personal branding expert, Dan Schawbel, writes in *The Five Laws of Being an Interesting Brand*, "Be yourself. Your personality is your best and most distinct attribute. I can't copy it, nor can any of my readers or anyone else in the world. It's easy to not be yourself sometimes because you want to impress someone or you want to fit in with cultural or group norms. When you start acting like everyone else, you lose the essence and beauty that would actually make people interested in you. By being yourself, you're bound to appeal to certain types of people."

Heretical thoughts, delivered in a way that capture the attention of the minority—that's the path that works.

- Seth Godin

3. Being different makes you **noticeable**. Being normal makes you **invisible**.

Fitting in makes us invisible. If we do things well, no one can see us. If we fit in at work, we don't get in trouble. We don't get fired, but we don't get promoted either. We don't get interesting projects and we don't get challenging tasks.

Average feels safe, but it's not. It's invisible.

- Seth Godin, *The Dip*

If our business fits in, everyone drives right by. No one stops. They don't know we're even there. If they do stop, they don't stay long and they don't buy anything because our products or services are just like everyone else's.

If we fit in, we don't get any attention. And attention is one of the most valuable gifts we can receive from others. Seth Godin, one of the world's most influential business bloggers, explained it this way in a message to his readers. "Every time you read something I write here, you're giving me a gift... attention. It's getting more precious all the time, you have more choices every day, and it's harder and harder to find the time. I know. I'm grateful. I'm doing my best to make your attention worth it."

Mark Sanborn is a well-known speaker and author of *The Fred Factor*, a story about an unusual mail carrier. Fred was different than most postal employees. He was so extraordinary that he got Mark's attention and ended up as the subject of a bestselling book. Fred's story teaches us an important lesson. As Sanborn said in a recent blog post, "we are bombarded by people and messages every day, all trying to get our attention. With limited attention, there is only so much we can give." People only take notice when something is unusual or surprising.

4. Being different makes you **surprising**. Being normal makes you **predictable**.

I was walking down the street in San Francisco and saw a homeless man with a cardboard sign, the kind that usually say "Will Work for Food" or "Homeless: Please Help." But this one didn't say anything predictable. It said "Who Am I Kidding? It's Miller Time!" As the Heath Brothers explain in *Made to Stick*:

The Freak Factor

Why Some Ideas Survive and Others Die, we are more likely to be persuaded by messages that are unexpected.

5. Being different makes you **memorable**. Being normal makes you **forgettable**.

We remember the unusual events in our lives, not the common ones. If no one remembers you or your message, then you don't have the opportunity to influence them. The worst criticism that Simon Cowell, the caustic judge of American Idol, can give is that a contestant is forgettable. In contrast, one of his most powerful compliments is that a contestant is memorable. He recently told one girl "You are such a strange person. I mean that as a compliment." We remember people that are strange.

6. Being different makes you **remarkable**. Being normal gives people **nothing to talk about**.

When we see something different, we want to tell other people about it. Once people remember you, the biggest challenge is getting them to tell others about you. As Mark Sanborn demonstrated, if you are remarkable enough, someone might even write a book about you. I regularly feature remarkable people on my blog as the Freak of the Week. Matt Langdon collects stories of everyday heroes and posts them on his blog. This word of mouth is powerful for individuals and businesses.

7. Being different makes you **influential**. Being normal makes you **impotent**.

If other people are sharing your message, it increases your influence because it enables you to reach a larger audience.

Strange and Significant

I'm a big Counting Crows fan. I've bought every one of their albums since the first one came out in college. Their newest release is *Saturday Nights and Sunday Mornings*, which includes the song *Insignificant*. The chorus includes the line, "I don't want to be so different but I don't want to be insignificant."

Lead singer/songwriter, Adam Duritz, seems to be saying that significance and difference are related and he fears that if he stops being different, he will stop being significant. I think this is a legitimate fear and acknowledges a real dilemma.

I also think too many of us are singing a different lyric. We're singing "I want to be significant but I don't want to be different." I don't think we really have a choice. I think they're connected. It seems that throughout history, significant figures have always been strange, they've been freaks.

Are you ready to be a freak? Are you ready to be different? Are you ready to be significant?

What Makes You Rare?

Being a freak is about being different, being unusual, being uncommon and being rare. At this point, it might be helpful to think about what makes you odd, atypical and exceptional. We tend to focus on the ways that we are similar to others. We want to be normal and we emphasize the characteristics that help us to fit in with everyone else. However, as we just discussed, this approach isn't very effective.

What is it about you that makes you different from most people? Here is my list:

- At a height of 6'6", I'm taller than 99% of people in the world. My tall stature might also contribute to greater reproductive success.

- I suffer from Morton's Toe. My second toe is longer than my first. Only 10% of the world's population has this condition.

- I've completed a marathon, a feat only accomplished by .10% of Americans.

- I'm the father of three daughters but no sons. I can't find the exact statistics on this but apparently it increases my risk of prostate cancer, wearing nail polish and watching Strawberry Shortcake cartoons.

- I have a very small neck, 14.5 inches. I know that this is unusual because I can't buy shirts with that size and the proper sleeve length at traditional stores. I have to buy my clothes online. The good news is that my pencil neck decreases my risk for heart disease and sleep apnea.

- I earned a doctor of management degree. 25% of Americans have graduated from college, 8% have graduate degrees and just 3% have doctorates.

- I'm a nerd. I listen to and read about 50 books per year. My record is 100. Most people don't do this. The average is four books per year. 27% percent don't read any books. Many of my fellow nerds are also older and female.

- I'm self-employed. This is unusual. Most people are employees. Depending on which report you look at, self-employed people make up less than 20% of the workforce.

The Freak Factor

Michelle Verhaeghe, a good friend and freelance designer, sent me this list of her rarities.

- I have "geographic tongue," a condition that occasionally causes white lines on my tongue forming random shapes, especially if I eat citrus. Only .06% of Americans have this condition and people like me make up 3% of the world's population.

- I wear socks to bed every night; I sleep terribly if I don't.

- I prefer the Mediterranean Food Pyramid as a guide for servings of food groups, rather than the American Heart Association Food Pyramid.

- As a female web designer, I am one of the less than 25% of women in the nation's IT industry.

What about you? What makes you rare? You can use the space below to create your list.

You might find distinctiveness in your appearance, personality, habits, accomplishments, career, education and/or family.

_____

_____

_____

_____

_____

_____

_____

_____

_____

A Bad Kid

I haven't always been proud of my strangeness. For most of my life I was unhappy because I couldn't fit in, wasn't well-rounded and couldn't conquer my weaknesses. So how did I find my own freak factor? How did I find the courage to be different?

A number of years ago my friend's wife, Lynn, asked me to do a parenting presentation for a women's group. I was happy to do the talk, but a little apprehensive. Because the meeting was just for women, I would be the only man in the room. Fifteen years of marriage and nine years of parenting three daughters has taught me that women don't like men to tell them how to do anything, much less how to take care of children.

To make matters worse, at the time of the presentation, I didn't have any children. My only qualifications were academic, since I had undergraduate and graduate degrees in counseling psychology. This probably wouldn't count for much since I already had two major strikes against me. I was a man with no children who telling mothers and grandmothers how to care for their offspring.

Fortunately, Lynn assured me that my failure to procreate would not be a problem. She had an introduction that would give me the credibility I needed to win over the audience. She started by listing my qualifications and then explained that I had been a friend of her husband's since high school. Apparently, he had shared many stories with her about my past and his revelations had led her to an important conclusion.

The final words of her introduction were, "The reason you should listen to Dave is because he is proof that even your really bad kids can turn out OK." Ouch! In other words, "He has seen behind the curtain. Listen up because he has secret knowledge about the inner workings of difficult children. Maybe he has some special insights to share from his checkered past." Her creative and light-hearted introduction broke the ice and the presentation went very well. However, this isn't a book about giving great introductions.

I want to focus on her final phrase. I'm a bad kid that turned out OK. How exactly did that happen? Was I really a bad kid? What lessons can we learn from that experience that will improve our work and our lives?

As Lynn suggested, I was indeed a bad kid, at least that's what everyone told me. My parents and teachers had three primary goals during my entire childhood. They wanted me to sit down, be quiet and do what I was told. My inability to master these basic skills was a major problem, especially since I was forced to spend most of my childhood in school, sitting still, listening and following instructions, or at least trying to. Because of my weaknesses, I was told repeatedly that I was obnoxious, immature, had a bad attitude and lacked self-control.

When I was in third grade, the principal called me into his office and sat me down on his lap. (This seems questionable in retrospect and I'm not sure if I've blocked out parts of that interaction). During our meeting, he told me about three kinds of people: bad people, really bad people and people that are so bad they won't be able to recover. He told me that I was really bad and almost too far gone. I was in third grade! I was only eight years old. I wasn't smoking weed behind the equipment shed. I was just a little disruptive.

The principal wasn't the only one who was frustrated with me. Even my parents called me motor-mouth because of my non-stop chatter. At one family gathering, one of my uncles, frustrated by my constant banter, told me to shut-up and accused me of being obnoxious. A few months later, in an ironic twist, my aunt divorced him. I guess maybe he was the obnoxious one.

One additional criticism, related to those I've already shared, was that I needed to be the center of attention. I was always telling jokes and getting people to focus on me. According to those in authority, this was a character flaw that needed correction.

You can only hear people tell you something is wrong with you for so long before you begin to believe them. I saw myself as immature, out of control, rebellious, hyperactive and unattractive, because others saw me that way. This didn't give me a lot of hope for my future and the problems continued throughout high school and into college. I did well for a while early in my career, but soon my distaste for authority, my hyperactivity and consistent failure to keep quiet continued to haunt me.

"This isn't working out," said Camille. "The problem is that you're just not a team player." Hearing this made me sick to my stomach. I was only a few weeks into my new job at a large nonprofit in Chicago. My former employer recently merged with another organization and I went from working mostly alone in a two-person operation to working with hundreds of people on a five-person team.

Now I was sitting in a booth at McDonalds' with my boss and two co-workers. They'd called this meeting to inform me that I needed to make some major changes in order to succeed in my new role. I was stunned. I had been very successful in my two previous jobs, which required me to work independently. This was my biggest strength and I thought that it would serve me well in my new position as well. But I was wrong.

It seemed like everything that was good about me was working against me. The very thing that my last boss praised me for, my ability to work independently, was about to cost me my job. My new co-workers saw me as a lone ranger. They complained that I didn't ask for their input and that I talked too much, too often and for too long in meetings. I didn't seem open to their involvement. Their organization valued teamwork very highly and if I couldn't change, they would ask me to leave.

Seeing the handwriting on the wall, I started looking for something new. I found a new job in a city closer to my family but was soon confronted with new challenges. My new responsibilities required me to create a brand-new business within an existing company. It was a perfect fit because I got to develop a plan for a dramatic change within the organization. The plan required a major investment of capital and created a lot of positive visibility for me and my company. After the new operation was in place, I was promoted to a senior management position and immediately began talking to my boss, the organization's CEO, about other change projects.

However, there was a conflict between my interest in starting new projects and the company's need for me to manage ongoing operations. There was also a conflict between my desire for rapid change and my boss's patient and deliberate approach. Our meetings gradually became more and more contentious as my boss continually admonished me to slow down and focus on improving existing processes and I argued for the need to speed up and dramatically transform the entire organization.

I strongly believed that I could do a better job of running the company. It was very difficult for me to follow someone with such a dramatically different approach. I'd never been very good at doing what I was told and I strongly valued freedom and the opportunity to control my own future.

Additionally, it was clear that some of my employees wanted me to provide more structure and specific direction. I was always talking about vision, mission, values and the long-term goals of my division but devoted little time to offering detailed instructions regarding short-term goals and daily activities. I believed that it was important to provide my employees with the autonomy to make these decisions. I thought that they had more insight into these issues than I did, since they were on the front lines every day.

Meetings were still a problem as well. I'm very intuitive and seemed to instantly develop a strong feeling about how the organization should proceed. Unfortunately, I couldn't always clearly articulate why I felt the way I did and I didn't necessarily present concrete evidence for the effectiveness of my recommendations. This didn't keep me from sharing my ideas very passionately and arguing for them strongly against challenges from others on the management team.

These issues began taking a toll on my health and happiness. I was constantly frustrated and irritable. I became very self-conscious and lost my confidence. My weight began to balloon as my eating habits and sleep patterns deteriorated. Every day at work was such a battle and I began to dread going into the office. I couldn't understand how my past success had turned into such a mess.

Eventually I resigned but even this went badly. I was asked to leave before my chosen resignation date because my boss and subordinates felt like I was no longer committed to the organization.

The Freak Factor

In summary, I had these weaknesses. I was:

- Too talkative. Not a good listener.
- Hyperactive. Not able to sit still.
- Too independent. Not a team player.
- Too intuitive. Not rational enough.
- Too passionate. Not calm enough.
- Too strategic. Not operational enough.
- Too focused on the future. Not focused enough on the present.
- Too impulsive. Not patient enough.

These seem like substantial challenges and a traditional approach to personal development would focus on fixing these weaknesses. However, I chose a different approach. I didn't improve by overcoming my weaknesses. I didn't really change myself at all. I succeeded by flaunting my weaknesses and finding situations that valued the positive side of my apparent flaws.

Instead of changing myself, I changed my situation. I quit my job as a manager and began working as a college professor. This change allowed me to teach two of my favorite subjects, managing change and strategy. I also started my own business, helping companies with strategic planning. My clients appreciate my strategic thinking and ability to help them see the big picture. They don't need me to be detail-oriented and focused on operations. They have that covered. They need me to help them look to the future and identify the larger issues that the organization was facing.

As a speaker, I get praised for my energy and enthusiasm. My passion is infectious and helps me connect with audiences. As a solo entrepreneur, I can change quickly and act on his intuition without having to convince others to follow. I can also work independently and don't need to be a team player. My initiative and obsession with achievement keeps me motivated without direction or supervision from others. I'm in control and I love it.

I'm rarely criticized any more for my weaknesses but I still have all the same flaws; they just don't matter in my new work.

I've also lost weight and started running marathons. I feel energized and confident. My work provides me with happiness and fulfillment and a sense that I have truly found my calling. My new career has been an unqualified success.

This unlikely transformation illustrates the seven strategies for finding your freak factor.

1. Awareness—Identify your strengths and weaknesses
2. Acceptance—Stop trying to fix your weaknesses
3. Appreciation—Embrace your unique characteristics
4. Amplification—Flaunt your weaknesses
5. Alignment—Find the right fit
6. Avoidance—Move out of situations that highlight your weaknesses
7. Affiliation—Partner with people who are strong where you are weak

1. **Awareness:** Identify Your Strengths and Weaknesses

During one of my management classes, I showed the DVD for *A Whole New Mind* by Daniel Pink. The following quote is from the introduction. "I think a great life is using your strengths, understanding what it is that you were put on this earth to do, understanding what it is that makes you unique, and what is the truest expression of who you are, doing that persistently in the service of something larger than yourself."

Do you know what you were put on this earth to do? Do you know what makes you unique? What is the truest expression of who you are? How could you combine all these things in the service of others? Our ability to build a fulfilling life begins with an awareness of our strengths and weaknesses, and an understanding of the unique value that we can add to the world.

2. **Acceptance:** Stop trying to fix your weaknesses

My wife and I recently watched *The Soloist*, a movie based on the true story of Los Angeles Times reporter, Steve Lopez and Nathaniel Ayers, a homeless man and musical prodigy who studied music at the Julliard School. At one point, Lopez is talking with the director of a homeless shelter about how to help Ayers. Lopez suggests that Ayers should undergo a psychiatric evaluation to discover what is wrong with him.

Director: I don't get too hung up on diagnosis.

Lopez: But how do you help somebody if you don't know what they have?

Director: Look at these people. Every one of them has been diagnosed more times than you can imagine and, as far as I can tell, it hasn't done them any good.

I agree. I think we are too hung up on diagnosing our own problems and the problems of others. Diagnosis usually doesn't do much good and it actually causes harm by making people believe that they are inadequate, flawed or damaged.

As I've already demonstrated, a century of traditional psychology hasn't done much to improve our mental health, happiness or fulfillment, but it has done a lot to brand people as broken and in need of repair. I think it is time for a new approach that focuses more on what is right with us and less on what is wrong with us.

Lopez comes to a similar realization at the end of the movie. At some point, he stops trying to fix Ayers and begins treating him like a friend. He stops trying to find what is wrong with his friend and° begins to accept him as a fellow human being. I think this is a good model for the rest of us to follow with ourselves, our spouses, children, friends, co-workers and employees.

3. Appreciation: Embrace your unique characteristics

There's nothing wrong with you. You will succeed because of your weaknesses, not in spite of them. You can find success in your apparent weaknesses because your biggest weaknesses are actually components of your biggest strengths. They are two sides of the same coin.

For example, in one recent study, 43% of respondents cited public speaking as their biggest fear. This is not an isolated result. In the American Institute of Psychology's annual study of people's biggest fears, public speaking was first on the list. Death was second, followed by long-term illness, snakes, spiders, bugs and flying. Apparently some people fear public speaking more than death.

Seinfeld explained it this way, "at any given funeral most people would rather be in the coffin than giving the eulogy." I love to make presentations. I love public speaking. Sometimes I speak in public, even when I shouldn't. This means that I love to do what most people would rather die than do. My desire to be the center of attention isn't a weakness; it is a strength. My longing to talk isn't a problem, it is an opportunity. And the same is true for your weaknesses.

4. Amplification: Flaunt your weaknesses

Amplification is the essence of flaunting your weaknesses. According to the Encarta Dictionary flaunt means "to parade yourself without shame. Show something off–to display something ostentatiously." This is a great description. Too often, we are uncomfortable with our weaknesses. We are ashamed of them, apologize for them and try to hide them. My goal in this book isn't simply to help you become comfortable with your weaknesses. I want you to parade them without shame. I want you to show them off.

I found a great example of amplification in a *Forbes* article about famous people who've been fired. One of them was Sue. After being fired, she said that she "discovered 'two things about myself: One, I'm not a good team player. And two, I'm not a good sport.' So, she chose the solitary occupation of novelist and thrived at it."

But it gets better. Sue has been married three times. During an especially ugly divorce and custody battle, she "would make herself feel better by imagining ways to kill or maim her ex-husband. Her fantasies were so vivid that she decided to write them down."

Sue Grafton is the author of the very successful alphabet series of mystery novels starting with *A is for Alibi*. Her writing career was based on her own violent fantasies. I guarantee that, if she had shared those cruel dreams with a medical professional, they would have given her medication. Instead, she turned her savage visions into a lifelong career as a writer. She's a great example of the power of amplification.

5. Alignment: Find the right spot

The fifth lesson is that we find success by finding the right fit. We need to connect who we are to situations and environments that reward us for our natural style and abilities, instead of punishing us. Too often we try to change ourselves to fit the situation. We try to become what the boss or teacher or coach or girl or guy wants us to be. I tried this for my whole life and it didn't work. Even six years of training to become a counselor didn't help me sit down and shut up. For years I'd been trying to change myself, when what I needed to do was change the situation. Everything turned around when I found activities that highlighted my innate strengths and made my many problems irrelevant.

For example, as a child, I was so skinny that you could see my heart beating… even when my shirt was on. When I graduated from high school, I was 6'4" and 145 pounds. Some of my nicknames during this time included twiggy, toothpick and walking stick. Twiggy was a female model from the 1960's known for her thin frame. I'm confident that it is every young man's dream to have his body compared to that of a woman. Crowds at basketball games would chant "walking stick" while I stood on the free throw line.

I desperately tried to gain weight by eating heavily and lifting weights but nothing worked. What I didn't know at the time was that I was an ectomorph. This is a body type characterized by the following features. Lest you think I'm making this up or exaggerating, I took this description directly from bodybuildingpro.com

- Delicately Built Body
- Flat Chest
- Fragile
- Lean
- Lightly Muscled
- Small Shouldered
- Takes Longer to Gain Muscle
- Thin

"The extreme ectomorph physique is a fragile and delicate one. The bones are light, joints are small and muscles are slight. The limbs are relatively long in proportion and the shoulders droop. The ectomorph is a linear physique. Straight up and straight down, and may appear longer than he or she really is, due to the length of limbs coupled with lack of muscle mass developed on those limbs. The ectomorph is not naturally powerful and will have to work hard for every ounce of muscle and every bit of strength he or she can gain."

Needless to say, this was not the kind of body that attracted the admiration of many ladies. The Body Building Pro website goes on to explain that "ectomorphs are generally better endurance athletes than bodybuilders by nature, and may excel in cross-country running." I didn't need to bulk up. I just needed to find a sport that fit who I already was.

Not only are ectomorphs ideally suited for distance running, it is difficult, if not impossible for those with larger body types to succeed in competitive running. The Stillman Table is one guide for the ideal height-to-weight ratio for runners. It recommends that long distance runners should weigh about two pounds for each inch of height. In other words, a runner who is six feet tall should weigh around 150 pounds.

Apparently, this ratio isn't just an academic or scientific recommendation. It seems to be consistent with the build of successful distance runners. Paul Tergat, who held the world record in the marathon from 2003 to 2007, is six feet tall and weighs just 137 pounds. This puts him at 1.9 pounds per inch. Tergat's record was broken by Haile Gebrselassie in September 2007 during the Berlin Marathon. Gebrselassie weighs in at a sturdy 123 pounds and is just five feet and three inches tall. This is almost exactly two pounds per inch. This physical requirement for running success rules out a lot of people in the same way that I'm excluded from being an offensive lineman for the Green Bay Packers.

I like the body type example because it is something that can't be changed. Additionally, it shows that my literal muscular weakness was actually a strength. However, it was only a strength when I found the right fit, distance running.

6. Avoidance: Move out of situations that highlight your weaknesses

Daniel Pink's book, *Johnny Bunko*, is the story of a struggling cubicle dweller that discovers six lessons of career success. Lesson #2 is "think strengths, not weaknesses." Johnny is working in the finance department, despite the fact that he loves art, learning about people and developing creative ideas. His job makes him miserable. However, instead of seeing that he is in the wrong spot, his solution is to get better at working with numbers and spreadsheets. He decides to take a series of training seminars to improve his skills.

His strategy is "to work harder… to get better at what I stink at… If I want to succeed, I need to focus where I'm weak and make sure that my weaknesses don't hold me back." As we've discussed, this is a very common approach and it usually fails.

Johnny's career advisor, Diana, suggests a new perspective. "Steer around your weaknesses and focus on your strengths. Successful people don't try too hard to improve what they're bad at. They capitalize on what they're good at." Johnny eventually finds greater fulfillment when he moves into a different role at the same company that doesn't require him to overcome his weaknesses in finance.

7. Affiliation: Partner with people who are strong where you are weak

If you stop doing the things you don't like to do, how will they get done? One option is to form relationships with people who have strengths that complement your weaknesses. You don't need to be well-rounded but you can still live a balanced life by finding the right people to help you.

One of my favorite examples of affiliation came from Sara Dunnigan at The Greater Richmond Partnership in Virginia.

"I've been struggling for weeks to write an annual report for a business program that I manage. Each year, we interview about 600 business people in an effort to connect them with resources and support the growth of their businesses. The annual report is an aggregate view of the data points and every time I tried to write an engaging, conversational report that people would actually want to read–it came out like a dry article from an economic journal. While well-written and chock full of facts and figures–this was not the effect I was going for.

This wasn't the first time I struggled with this project. It has been my responsibility for more than three years and no matter what I did to get better (I must have read every other similar publication in the country) I just couldn't get there. In fact, during the time I spent trying to write, all I really wanted to do was go out and talk to stakeholders in the community about what we had discovered, what we had done and exciting plans for the future."

After struggling to write the report on her own for years, she finally tried a different approach.

"I had been working with Grace, an intern in our office who was a fantastic writer. I did the data gathering and roughed in the outline and she reorganized the content and added the dimensional writing I was looking for in the project. I'm happy because now I get to focus on building on my skills as a speaker and solutions facilitator and Grace got to use her skills and add another great project to her portfolio. Now I am excited about using this approach for other projects our small team works on."

Finding someone else to write the report was a win-win-win situation. Sara was happy because she had more time to do what she loved. Her company and constituents were happy because the report was more interesting and Grace was happy because she had an opportunity to use her strengths at work. Affiliation enhances teamwork and improves performance.

Throughout the rest of the book, I'll devote a chapter to each of these seven strategies. Mary's story, below, shows how these strategies can transform your life.

Freak Profile: Mary Sailors

Mary contacted me after reading *The Freak Factor* manifesto. Her boss gave it to her and Mary liked what she read so much that she decided to quit her job. That's probably not the response her boss was hoping for.

Mary now works as a personal trainer and specialty fitness instructor in Minneapolis, Minnesota. She is also a healthy lifestyle blogger, writing at **www.fitthisgirl. com**. When she's not train-ing clients, she volunteers with Bolder Options, a youth mentorship program in Minneapolis. She just ran her first marathon in Honolulu. You can find her on Twitter @ fitthisgirl.

"I have always colored out-side the lines. As a child, I struggled with the confines of a classroom, with doing work and with having to fit into any kind of mold, except for the one I made myself. But when I graduated from college, I fell into a job, at an office, in a cubicle. I felt important, adult, professional, like I was doing what I should do.

Years passed and I moved from one office to the next, from one set of gray walls to the next. I made slight advances, as much as a literature major in Corporate America can. I kept changing titles, but always kept 'assistant' on the end, like a tag line. I was excelling at being mediocre. I was barely getting by, lacking in joy and feeling inadequate. The problem wasn't just the jobs I was working, but also my performance in them.

What was wrong with me? I was a smart, passionate and vibrant free-thinker and I could screw up an office supply order with the best of them. Then I found something that I really could do well—working a front desk, greeting people, and being the face of a company! I excelled. I was given more responsibility and started to struggle with the expectations. I started to examine the things I fell short on, the projects that I procrastinated on, the tasks that I screwed up.

Did I have ADD? ADHD? Did I have a bad attitude?

But the woman I worked for saw my full potential. One time, when talking about a certain project, she asked me, 'Who told you that you weren't capable?' Then she handed me a copy of *The Freak Factor* manifesto. What I read changed the way that I looked at myself and my work.

If you are anything like me then you probably have an idea of what your weakness are. As much as I wish I had fewer weaknesses, I don't really intend to go through life sweeping them under the rug or making excuses for them like I had been up to that point. I learned to look at my weakness a little differently after reading the Freak Factor.

I needed to shift my focus. Weaknesses are not always bad thing. Instead of focusing on overcoming our weaknesses, we can harness the corresponding strength to achieve our potential in our life, work and relationships.

Most people focus on their weaknesses and work hard on turning them into strengths. I was working hard trying to improve where I fell short, trying to find fixes and shortcuts and ways to work better. For a while, it worked. Things got a little better, but I was hammering my weakness into submission only to end up with a slightly dented version of the original product.

The main key to succeeding by finding the strengths hiding inside your weaknesses is to seek out situations where you can use your strengths and excel there. If you are constantly in situations where you are required to use your weaknesses you will not feel like you are succeeding. When you feel that, examine the situation and ask 'why don't I feel successful here?' You will be able to pinpoint corresponding strengths more easily when you see your weaknesses for what they are.

The Freak Factor

I learned to choose situations that fit my natural strengths. That meant a career change. I researched becoming a personal trainer, did the work and leaped out into a world of the unknown. I moved from a well paying corporate job, which I was mediocre at, into unpaid internships and a world where I was able to tap into my strengths and use my natural skills to excel.

I have been working as a personal trainer for only eight months and have already been praised by my boss as being a 'professional highlight.' I've been encouraged to never lose my natural love and enthusiasm for people and training. I've also received countless positive comments. I don't say this to say 'look at me and what I have done!' What I'm trying to say is that when you are working from your true strengths, it will be apparent."

I was so excited about Mary's transformation that I wanted to learn more. Below are her answers to a few of my follow-up questions.

Tell me more about particular weaknesses and how you discovered the strengths that corresponded with them?

I was never built to sit still. As a receptionist I was always confined to a front desk and copy room. I felt restless and agitated and that made me feel unproductive. I actually was unproductive too. I would start projects, get bored and leave them half done. It wasn't that I was bored with the project itself, I was bored with my inability to move around in my position and bored with the confinement of my job. I would have multiple projects half completed and no motivation to finish any of them.

Weaknesses that I discovered on that job were only weaknesses within that environment. In a different setting they could easily be strengths. For instance, when someone would request a project or special order from me, I would just dive right in and have to back pedal later. In hindsight, I can see the value in asking all the important questions up front, but my enthusiastic drive was never tapped in the way it is in some of my current ventures.

What weaknesses did you struggle with on the job? Were you disorganized, unfocused, hyperactive, etc?

I had to work extra hard to be organized in the way that the rest of the team required. There was little room for individual style in my work. As a personal trainer, I still have to do paperwork, like tracking client progress, planning sessions, follow-up and notes. The difference is that I am free to do it on my own time and in my own way. It's a much more creative environment.

0. awakening

Did you find any of your weaknesses on the strength/weakness chart? YES!

Positive-Unrealistic: My head is always in the clouds.

Passionate-Impatient: Oh how I want things right now!

Creative-Unorganized

Dedicated-Stubborn

Enthusiastic-Obnoxious

* This chart is in Chapter 2—Acceptance

What is it about being a trainer that matches your unique strengths?

One of my strengths is that I have a heart for serving and helping people. I'm also good at showing people how to do things the best way. I'm a natural leader and planner, but due to some situations in life, I adopted more of a follower approach. Sitting behind a desk as a receptionist or in a cube kept me from being able to lead. I may have been the face of the organization, but I didn't have the opportunity to lead or use the true power that I knew I had. My strength was never in administrative duties. I excelled much more in the personal and social aspects. Now, as a trainer, I have the opportunity to lead and direct individuals and groups.

Mary was lucky to have a boss who saw the strengths hiding inside of her weaknesses.

I was fortunate to have someone like that in my life as well. Late in my sophomore year of college, Elliott Anderson, the resident director of the men's dorm approached me and asked me to apply for a resident assistant position. This was a big surprise. Up to this point, I thought I was the reason that the college employed resident assistants. I saw myself as a rule breaker, not a member of the enforcement team. However, Elliott saw something else.

He saw a lot of himself when he looked at me. He was also a bad kid that turned out OK. Maybe he could help. It was great to work with him and we are still friends today. He was the first one to call me freak, which is one of the few nicknames I am proud of and was the inspiration for the title of this book.

1. awareness

weaknesses are important clues to your strengths

We are led to truth by our weaknesses as well as our strengths.

- Parker Palmer, *Let Your Life Speak*

The goal of this chapter is to define a few key terms and help you identify your unique strengths and weaknesses.

Freak

The July 7, 2008 cover of Sports Illustrated simply said "The Freak" next to a picture of Tim Lincecum, a pitcher for the San Francisco Giants. They call him a freak because he is just 5'10" and weighs only 170 pounds. In contrast, the average pitcher in Major League Baseball is over six feet tall and weighs closer to 200 pounds. Lincecum isn't normal. As Mike Powell explains, "The normal stride length for a pitcher is 77% to 87% of his height. Lincecum's stride is 129%, or roughly 7.5 feet."

Tim's father, Chris, wasn't particularly excited about his son being called a freak and called Tim to talk about it.

"Tim, everybody is calling you a freak."

"Well, Dad, I am. Why?"

"How can you say you're a freak? You're just a good athlete."

"O.K., is Michael Jordan a freak? Tiger Woods? Jack Nicklaus?"

"Yeah, I'd consider them freaks," Chris said. "Then, O.K., you're a freak."

However, not everyone is excited about working with freaks. A lot of teams refused to draft Lincecum because of his unusual stature and unconventional pitching style. "One guy (scout) said his mechanics were unorthodox, and people ran with it." It was their loss.

The freak won the Cy Young award in 2008 and 2009. The next time Lincecum was on the cover of Sports Illustrated was two years later in the final issue of 2010. The headline was "Get Your Freak On" and he was pictured celebrating the Giants' World Series victory, in which the little guy with the weird delivery won two games.

Tim Lincecum is an interesting example, but what exactly does it mean to be a freak?

The term freak can mean maniac, fanatic, something unusual, irregular or abnormally formed, an eccentric or nonconformist person, or a person who is obsessed with something. In this book I define a freak as a person who is unique because of a natural positive obsession. I use the word as a compliment. However, being a freak wasn't always considered a good thing.

Sign says long-haired freaky people need not apply.

– Five Man Electrical Band, *Signs*

The Wikipedia entry for freak explains that "a freak is often considered a pejorative term for an organism with an abnormality of some kind. The older usage, referring to the physically deformed, such as that would be seen in a sideshow, has generally fallen into disuse." Notice that freak used to be a negative label. I purposely chose the term because of its history and ambiguous meaning.

Unique

"In current usage, the word freak denotes a person with an unusual personality." This meaning is consistent with my use of the word. As we discussed previously, being a freak means being different.

Unfortunately, instead of embracing our uniqueness, we often try to hide it in an effort to be more normal. This is because many people discourage our uniqueness by framing it as a weakness. That leads us to the next part of the definition.

"The word is still used when describing mutations in plants and animals, but more often is applied to humans."

I think the idea of mutation is also a helpful one. Mutants are weird, strange and bizarre.

"A freak can be formally defined as someone not falling within typical standard deviations. For example, people of small stature would not be classified as freaks unless they are within the third standard deviation for the general population, while the same principle would apply to exceptionally tall people."

I like the final part of the definition because, as an "exceptionally tall" person, it officially classifies me as a freak.

Positive

"The word freak, when used in a slang context, also has positive connotations. The term can be used to describe one who is unusually skilled or talented in a particular area."

This is my favorite part. I intend to use freak in a positive way. I think it is good to be a freak and I want to encourage you to feel the same way. Who wouldn't want to be "unusually skilled or talented?"

The real success goes to those who obsess.

- Seth Godin, *The Dip*

Obsession

"Freak can also mean someone who is utterly obsessed with… a particular activity."

Steve Almond is a fellow ectomorph and the author of *Candy Freak*, a hilarious and fascinating book about his obsession with candy. In it, he describes his travels across the country exploring the inner workings of famous and obscure purveyors of sweet delights. His book and his life definitely illustrate the positive aspects of obsession. Despite the fact that his obsession is candy, he is very philosophical. He thinks of freak as a verb, an active desire.

"We don't choose our freaks. They choose us… We may not understand why we freak on a particular food or band or sports team. We may have no conscious control over our allegiances. But they arise from our most sacred fears and desires, and, as such they represent the truest expression of our selves." When you read Almond's descriptions of his experiences with candy, you can feel his unrestrained passion and you almost start to feel the same way.

Steve illustrates the positive elements of obsession. His writing makes it obvious that he has embraced his freakness and he flaunts it on each and every page. For example, one section discusses candy porn and another explores his oral fixation. Despite his constant candy consumption, he is able to maintain a slim physique. This is due to his ectomorph body type. Steve has found a great fit between his addiction and his natural build.

Natural

"Freaks can be classified into two groups... natural freaks and made freaks. A natural freak would refer to a genetic mutant, while a made freak is a once normal person who experienced or initiated an alteration at some point in life."

The goal of this book is to help you discover and enhance your natural freakness. I don't think any of us are, or were, normal and most of us don't have to go to the trouble of making ourselves into freaks. We just came that way. As Almond said, "We don't choose our freaks, they choose us." I hope this book with help you to accept and appreciate your innate qualities.

The idea of a "made" freak is also helpful. I'd like to help you make yourself into a bigger freak than you already are. As Marcus Buckingham says in *First Break All the Rules*, "don't try to put in what was left out, try to draw out what was left in." This sentiment is echoed by Tom Rath of the Gallup Organization. He believes that "you can't be anything you want to be, but you can be more of who you are." That really crystallizes the purpose of this book, to help you to become more of who you are.

Strength

While we're defining terms, it is probably important to clarify the meanings of the terms strength and weakness. The Gallup Organization is the leader of what they call the "strengths revolution," an application of positive psychology to individual and organizational performance. They define strength as "the ability to consistently produce a nearly perfect positive outcome in a specific task." This is a good definition, but it is too specific for our purposes.

Their definition of talent is closer to what I mean by strength. Gallup describes talents as "a recurring pattern of thought, feeling or behavior that can be productively applied." When I talk about strengths in this book, this is what I mean.

I define strength as a pattern of passion and proficiency. Strengths are patterns because they describe how we usually, consistently, or regularly feel or act. Strengths aren't things that we sometimes do, occasionally like or rarely experience. This is like the difference between a solitary action and a habit. Actions are isolated events, while habits are patterns.

Passion means that you love something. You can't wait for activities that allow you to exercise your strengths and you are energized by participating in those activities. Too often, self-improvement programs focus on perseverance and discipline, while neglecting passion. However, a basic understanding of human nature shows us that people do what makes them feel good and avoid actions that make them feel bad. This is why the "no-pain, no-gain" philosophy leads to so much frustration.

I believe that passion creates perseverance. We dedicate ourselves to those things that we enjoy, that make us feel good. Those positive emotions carry us through times of potential difficulty or struggle. I don't think that many people successfully persevere to accomplish goals that they don't want or to engage in activities they don't like.

Proficiency means that you have a natural talent in this area. You are good at it. You have had success in the past and you anticipate success in the future. Ability is essential to motivation. According to expectancy theory, we will not be motivated to do something unless we can answer yes to all of the following three questions.

   1. Can I do it?   2. Will I be rewarded?   3. Do I value the reward?

Notice the first question. If you don't think that you can do something, it doesn't matter what rewards are offered. Motivation requires ability or at least the perception that you have the ability. However, ability and proficiency aren't the same as perfection. There are always opportunities to build on our strengths and this is not the same as fixing a weakness.

For example, I run marathons. I love to run. I love being alone. I love the feeling of achievement as the miles pass. I love being in motion. I love the way it feels to cross the finish line. I also have natural gifts in this area.

As we discussed earlier, my body type is ideal for distance running. I'm also a task and goal-oriented person. I'm good at setting and achieving objectives. I've always been hyperactive, which led to an interest in sports. I have always been above average in my athletic pursuits including golf, basketball and baseball. However, despite my proficiency, I can still improve.

I ran my first marathon in February 2005 and felt a great deal of pride for finishing. Six months earlier, I wasn't exercising at all. My only vigorous activity involved running to the car if it was raining. During my marathon training, I lost 40 pounds and I felt great. Additionally, an internet search revealed that less than 0.1% of Americans will ever complete a marathon (26.2 miles). My accomplishment put me into an elite group. I was feeling good, but only for a while.

At most distance races, runners are given a computer chip that tracks their progress, records their time and helps to deter cheating. It also makes it possible for race organizers to almost instantaneously upload race results to their website. These results list the top three finishers in each age/gender category and then provide a list of every person's finishing time.

My time was 4:28:43. The race winner finished almost two hours before me. I knew this because I watched him run past mile 25, while I was crossing mile 14. That was not an encouraging moment.

As I browsed through the age group winners online, I saw that I was slower than the top runner in almost every age and gender category. The top man and top woman in each category finished faster than I did. From the 20-24 year old men and women to the 25-29 year old male and female winners, up through those in their 30's, 40's and 50's, I didn't beat anyone. I wasn't feeling so good anymore. But I had hope. Surely I'd beaten the senior citizens, at least the senior women. But it was not to be.

The winner of the 60-64 year old men's group finished in 3:10:31, more than an hour before me. The female winner of this group also beat me by four minutes. The next men's age group winner (65-69) also arrived before me. However, I can proudly say that I was faster than the female winner in that category! But even this victory was short lived. I soon discovered that she was the only participant in that category.

There was only one age group left, 70-99 years old. The male winner, age 77, finished almost 30 minutes before I did. The second place man, age 72, got me by 15 minutes. My only redemption came in the ladies division of the 70-99 age group. My time was more than an hour better than the female winner. Again, though, she was one of only two racers in this group.

I was dumbfounded and demoralized. I'd been beaten by a 64-year old woman and a 77-year old man. I hadn't even seen these old-timers on the course but this is probably because they were so far in front of me.

In 2006, I improved my time by 15 minutes, but the results were almost identical to the previous year. The only difference was my domination of the 70-99 year old men's category. Unfortunately, I was 32 at the time. To make matters worse, the 70+ men came back with a vengeance and regained their crown in 2007.

I had another bad experience in that race. A woman passed me just before mile 26. There was a laminated sign pinned to the back of her shirt. It read "I'm not slow, I'm just pregnant." I never saw her again. A woman who was great with child left me in the dust! In case you think I'm making this up or exaggerating for effect, you can visit the Myrtle Beach Marathon website and view the results.

My humiliation doesn't end there. In late 2006, I ran the Outer Banks Marathon in a driving rainstorm. Struggling to continue as my shoes filled with water and felt like lead weights, I did manage to keep running. Apparently, running isn't exactly the right term for what I was doing though. Late in the race I was surprised to see an older woman pass me. She was power-walking. I didn't ever catch up to her.

In October 2007, I attempted my first ultra-marathon, a 40-mile trail race in Greensboro, North Carolina. My finishing time was 9:15:36, which was good enough to put me in the top 50. I was just glad to finish. Unfortunately, my top 50 showing doesn't seem as impressive when you consider that there were only 54 runners in the race. At mile 38, I got passed by a woman and a 63-year old man. I never saw them again. The winner of the race finished almost four hours ahead of me and another 61-year old man completed the race nearly two hours faster.

In November of 2007, I ran the Richmond Marathon with my sister-in-law, who was attempting her first marathon. While crossing a long bridge, we were passed by a man who was juggling five balls as he was running. We never caught up to him.

My in-laws were at the race and met us at various spots along the course. They explained that they knew we would be coming along soon when they saw certain runners who were always a few minutes ahead of us. One of these runners was a blind woman being led by a guide. We never caught up to her either.

Here's the point. I'm built for running. I'm good at it and I enjoy it. However, I still have a lot of room for improvement. I can still continue to build on this strength. Despite my many humiliations, running is not a weakness. I don't need to fix my running weaknesses. I need to build on the existing strengths that I have.

Weakness

I define weakness as a pattern of apathy, aversion or failure. Each of these words is important. We've already discussed the definition of a pattern. Apathy means that you have no interest in this area. You don't necessarily dislike it. You just don't care. Aversion, on the other hand, means that you find the activity offensive or repulsive. You have an active distaste for it. Weaknesses usually drain us. We become exhausted when forced to do things in areas of weakness.

Failure means that you have a lack of ability and have consistently struggled with it in the past. Notice that I used or, instead of and, in the definition. As we'll discuss later, the presence of apathy, aversion or failure is enough to create a weakness, since any one of these is enough to limit your potential for success.

For example, many of the initial contestants on American Idol have a passion for music. They love music. However, they lack ability in this area. Passion alone is necessary but not sufficient.

I have the same problem with music. I love it. I listen to my iPod when I run and have music on all day while I work. Great music energizes me and lifts me up. Because I love the spotlight, I'd love to be a lead singer in a band. Because I'm hyperactive, being a drummer is very attractive to me. Unfortunately, I have no musical ability.

I discovered this truth in college. Back then, I believed in the importance of being well-rounded, being a Renaissance Man. To that end, I enrolled in piano lessons. I dropped the class after trying in vain to finish one of my first elementary assignments. Playing "Mary had a Little Lamb" with one finger on the piano was beyond my capabilities.

Undaunted, I enrolled in voice lessons. With no experience in singing, the instructor immediately began trying to teach me "The Impossible Dream" from the musical, Man of La Mancha. Impossible was an apt description of the song, at least as far as I was concerned. The lessons ended and so did my hopes for a career as a lead singer.

Next, I tried to learn guitar from my friend. Unfortunately, my left arm is mildly deformed due to a severe break as a child and I am unable to hold the guitar correctly. My arm also gives me a lot of trouble when I'm picking up fast food at the drive-thru. I could have tried to play with the other hand, but, given my existing musical disabilities, that would have only compounded my problems. The legacies of Jimi Hendrix and Eric Clapton are safe.

After my college basketball career was ended by a back injury, I had a lot of time on my hands. Some of my friends were in choir and asked me to join. However, I had to audition first, with the same instructor that participated in my voice lesson debacle. He was a short, kind and sincere older gentleman. After I sang the audition piece, in front of everyone else, he had this to say. "David, there are some people that the choir needs and there are some people who need the choir." Long pause. "David, I think you need the choir." I was in!

Getting into the choir was my only achievement. The class was graded on a pass/fail basis and the only requirement for passing the class was attendance. My work schedule made it difficult for me to make all of the rehearsals. However, I had an advantage in this area, since I was dating the choir attendance secretary at the time. Unfortunately, she took her job more seriously than our relationship. Despite my charms, she maintained the integrity of her sacred duty and recorded each of my absences. I failed the class but it wasn't a total loss. I've been married to the choir attendance secretary for the last 15 years. She still refuses to cut me any slack. She is also responsible for any musical training that our children might receive. Her college major was music performance.

I should also explain that there were earlier clues to my lack of potential in the musical realm. When other people in a group would clap along with a particular song, I was unable to get started, or, once started, to stay with the rhythm. It was like waiting to hop into an active session of double-dutch. There never seemed to be an opening and once I got in, the jump ropes got all tangled around me. My wife explained that I was trying to clap on the off-beat, but I don't know what that means. I just keep my hands in my pockets. Needless to say, this was the nail in the coffin of my drumming dreams.

The fact that I have no rhythm also hurts my performance on the dance floor. Growing up, I went to private religious schools. They frowned upon dancing and saw it as "vertical intercourse." We had banquets and dinners instead of proms and formals. This significantly impeded my dancing development.

The Freak Factor

Combined with my other musical deficiencies, I am a danger to myself and others while attempting to dance. My wife and I were almost seriously injured while attempting to dance at my brother's wedding. This was mostly my fault, but my wife does bear some of the responsibility.

My wife and I have a major height mismatch. She is 5'3" and I am 6'6". If that is hard for you to picture, just consider that, in our relationship, deodorant is more important than breath mints. Our height difference is enough to qualify ours as a mixed marriage, just the same as if we were different in race, religion, culture, etc. As you can imagine, we draw a lot of attention in public, not to mention when we are dancing. You won't see us on Dancing with the Stars any time soon.

The lesson from all of this is simple. I love music but it is not one of my strengths. It is a weakness because, even though I have passion, I lack any musical ability. I don't even have a small foundation of potential to build upon.

Learn what you are and be such.

- Pindar, *The Odes*

Self-Awareness

I'm not a huge *American Idol* fan. I enjoy the first few episodes where some really bad singers are allowed to audition but then my interest fades. However, besides the entertainment value of some of these dreadful performances, we can also learn important lessons from the tone-deaf contestants.

Many motivational speakers encourage their audience to "do what you love" and "pursue your passions." That seems like good advice but it is only the beginning of good advice. Think about it. In order to appear on American Idol, a potential contestant has to travel to the host city (one girl sold her horse in order to pay for a ticket from Oregon to Pennsylvania), wait for hours or days, sometimes in the extreme heat or cold, in large stadiums or parking lots with just a faint hope of even being seen by the judges, much less being selected for the next round.

It is safe to assume that most of these people love music. They love singing and they are passionate about what they do. Some of them are even trying to fulfill their dreams by singing in bars or restaurants or teaching music lessons.

Unfortunately, most of them lack talent. They are terrible singers. They have bad voices. It is painful to listen to them and no amount of passion can overcome that problem.

1. awareness

I think there is an important lesson that we can learn from American Idol. It is important to know what your strengths and weaknesses are. I am mystified by the lack of self-awareness exhibited by some of these aspiring stars. It isn't that they aren't good enough to be the next American Idol; they are so bad that they shouldn't be allowed to perform on karaoke night at a local bar. If they knew, or were willing to admit, that they lacked the ability to sing, they could focus on other activities where they had more potential.

This chapter is based on the belief that improving your self-awareness can improve your effectiveness.

Twenty Questions

Below is a list of questions to help you discover your strengths and weaknesses. I encourage you to take some time to consider each of them before moving to the next section. The following chapters assume that you have a strong awareness of your strengths and weaknesses. These questions will help you develop or improve that awareness.

1. What is the **biggest success** that I've ever had?

2. What was the **happiest day** of my life? What was I doing? Who was I with?

3. What was my **favorite class** in school? Which part did I like best?

4. What do others **consistently praise me** for?

5. What activities **energize** me? When do I lose track of time?

6. What was my **favorite job?** What did I like about it?

7. What is the **biggest failure** that I've ever experienced?

8. What was my **least favorite class** in school? Which part did I dislike the most?

9. What do others **consistently criticize me** for?

10. What activities **drain my energy?**

11. What do I **wish I could change** about myself?

The Freak Factor

12. Which tasks do I tend to **procrastinate?**

13. What was my **worst job?** What did I hate about it?

14. How can I **build on my strengths?**

15. How can I **flaunt my weaknesses?** How can I do more of what people tell me not to do? (we'll discuss this more in the chapter on amplification)

16. How can I **do the opposite** of what everyone else is doing? (we'll discuss this more in the chapter on amplification)

17. Who can I work with that is **strong where I am weak?** (we'll discuss this more in the chapter on affiliation)

18. What situations **spotlight my strengths** and make my weaknesses irrelevant? (we'll discuss this more in the chapter on alignment)

19. How can I **stick out** instead of trying to fit in?

20. How can I **stop doing** activities that drain me and replace them with those that energize me? (we'll discuss this more in the chapter on avoidance)

It's up to each of us alone to figure out who we are, who we are not, and to act more or less consistently with those conclusions.

- Tom Peters

Your Strengths

It can be difficult to answer fill-in-the-blank questions. Sometimes it is easier when questions are multiple-choice. That is why I created extensive lists of potential strengths and weaknesses.

As you identify your strengths, put a check in the box on the left next to your positive characteristics. Once you've done this, choose your top five strengths and rank them from one to five (one being the strongest). If you notice any characteristics that are definitely not a strength, draw a line through them.

X	STRENGTHS	RANK
1.	Creative, Innovative	
2.	Organized, Systematic	
3.	Dedicated, Persistent	
4.	Flexible, Adaptable	
5.	Enthusiastic, Passionate	
6.	Calm, Laid-Back	
7.	Dynamic, Active	
8.	Reflective, Thoughtful	
9.	Adventurous, Courageous	
10.	Responsible, Cautious	
11.	Activist, Revolutionary	
12.	Conventional, Traditional	
13.	Direct, Honest	
14.	Polite, Courteous	
15.	Cooperative, Helpful	
16.	Competitive, Assertive	
17.	Theoretical, Idealistic	
18.	Realistic, Practical	
19.	Independent, Self-Sufficient	
20.	Team Player, Unselfish	

X STRENGTHS	RANK
21. Objective, Unbiased	
22. Sensitive, Caring	
23. Humble, Modest	
24. Confident, Secure	
25. Patient, Cautious	
26. Spontaneous, Instinctive	
27. Influential, Powerful	
28. Obedient, Dutiful	
29. Motivated, Ambitious	
30. Relaxed, Easygoing	
31. Analytical, Rational	
32. Compassionate, Sympathetic	
33. Positive, Encouraging	
34. Realistic, Sensible	
35. Open-Minded, Tolerant	
36. Certain, Decisive	
37. Extravagant, Elegant	
38. Simple, Natural	
39. Self-Controlled, Disciplined	
40. Fun, Entertaining	
41. Serious, Mature	
42. Funny, Amusing	
43. Focused, Diligent	
44. Exploring, Discovering	
45. Generous, Altruistic	
46. Frugal, Thrifty	
47. Curious, Inquisitive	
48. Content, Satisfied	
49. Loyal, Devoted	
50. Adaptable, Flexible	
51. Detail-Oriented, Meticulous	
52. Global, General	

Your Weaknesses

As you identify your weaknesses, put a check in the box on the left next to your negative characteristics. Once you've done this, choose your top five weaknesses and rank them from one to five (one being the weakest). If you notice any characteristics that are definitely not a weakness, draw a line through them.

X	WEAKNESSES	RANK
1.	Chaotic, Disorganized	
2.	Rigid, Inflexible	
3.	Stubborn, Obstinate	
4.	Inconsistent, Unreliable	
5.	Quick-Tempered, Angry	
6.	Unfeeling, Emotionless	
7.	Frantic, Restless	
8.	Quiet, Shy	
9.	Reckless, Irresponsible	
10.	Boring, Uninteresting	
11.	Rebellious, Radical	
12.	Old-Fashioned, Conformist	
13.	Blunt, Rude	
14.	Superficial, Insincere	
15.	Passive, Submissive	
16.	Antagonistic, Aggressive	
17.	Unrealistic, Impractical	
18.	Negative, Critical	
19.	Isolated, Selfish	
20.	Dependent, Needy	
21.	Detached, Insensitive	
22.	Vulnerable, Emotional	
23.	Timid, Insecure	
24.	Arrogant, Conceited	
25.	Slow, Indecisive	

X WEAKNESSES	RANK
26. Impatient, Impulsive	
27. Controlling, Manipulative	
28. Weak, Subservient	
29. Obsessive, Workaholic	
30. Unmotivated, Lazy	
31. Critical, Judgmental	
32. Lenient, Indulgent	
33. Flattering, Naive	
34. Negative, Discouraging	
35. Unprincipled, Naive	
36. Opinionated, Dogmatic	
37. Complicated, Difficult	
38. Plain, Dull	
39. Harsh, Stiff	
40. Hedonistic, Self-Indulgent	
41. Humorless, Solemn	
42. Silly, Immature	
43. Limited, Restricted, Narrow	
44. Distractible, Unfocused	
45. Pushover, Sucker	
46. Stingy, Cheap	
47. Intrusive, Nosy	
48. Apathetic, Indifferent	
49. Robotic, Gullible	
50. Disloyal, Fickle	
51. Perfectionist, Compulsive	
52. Sloppy, Careless	

At this point, most self-help books would encourage you to use your newfound aware-ness to fix your weaknesses. That is the exact opposite of what I'm going to recommend. I don't want you to fix your weaknesses. I want you to accept them and to discover that your weaknesses are important clues to your strengths. That is the subject of the next chapter on acceptance. But before we move on, let's find out how Matthew Peters discov-ered his freak factor.

Freak Profile: Matthew Peters

Matthew is the author of *Don't Own, Don't Rent, Live Well*. I met him a couple months ago at a seminar. He's got a great freak factor story and I asked him if he'd be willing to share it.

"Since I was just a kid, I knew I was different. As my classmates excelled, I lagged way behind because I would sit in school 'daydreaming,' drawing pictures, inventing con-traptions or figuring out how I could buy candy bars for a quarter and sell them at school for fifty-cents.

It all started when I was seven years old and my parents explained to me how I could go out to our corn field, pick sweet corn, and sell it out of my dad's pickup truck by the highway. The traffic was good and everyone that stopped bought from me. I had to learn

The Freak Factor

to market by putting up signs. I had to educate the customer about my product and use math to count and make change for their large bills. Thankfully, the product sold itself and my costs were zero.

On the farm I did chores for a couple dollars a week, but selling sweet corn was different. I realized that I could make in one day what my brother and sister and I were making in a couple weeks of chores.

Back in the church basement classroom, my mind reeled as to how I could make even more money. To set the scene for you, we worked at our own pace in our little desks with dividers on either side while facing a tan concrete block wall for six hours a day. This was not the best learning environment for a kid with big dreams and an active imagination.

I wasn't interested in studying spelling, math or following the rules in general. I just wanted to come up with more ideas of how I could make more money using pure ingenuity. My enterprises were frowned upon by the church-school administration. I was shut down multiple times because I was selling candy, soda, stickers and iron-ons on school property. I didn't understand why my parents promoted it and the school took disciplinary action because of it. But it didn't stop me.

I cared so little about school that I should have failed second and third grades, but thanks to Mrs. Hansen, I passed since she believed I was a 'good kid.' Today, I'm one of those 'jobless' statistics you've read and heard about so much. I was a great employee because whatever I do, I give my best, but I haven't actually held a job since quitting my cushy university position in 2002.

A while back, I decided to follow my weaknesses and now I happily create interactive, video-based educational materials. I design and build websites, produce digital and tangible products, and teach people how to beat the system (or at least challenge conventional thought). My main focus lately is teaching people how to escape the binary trap of owning a home or renting one.

Though I still consider myself a poor speller, I have written a book about how my wife and I have taken the idea of paying nothing for our housing for over 9 years and developed it into a system of freedom, flexibility and opportunity that only a rare few have achieved. My Community Executive Academy teaches people how to get out of debt, put more of their hard-earned money toward their future and live life on their own terms instead of that of others by helping them recoup all of the money they were spending on their housing. I owe a debt of gratitude to my parents who all along encouraged me to follow my 'weaknesses.'

2. acceptance

apparent weaknesses are strengths in disguise

I now know myself to be a person of weakness and strength, liability and giftedness, darkness and light. I now know that to be whole means to reject none of it but to embrace all of it.

— Parker Palmer, *Let Your Life Speak*

In the previous chapter on awareness, I offered strategies for uncovering and understanding your strengths and weaknesses. Once we are aware of our weaknesses we need to resist the impulse to correct them. The second step in maximizing your freak factor is to accept the inevitability of weaknesses and identify the strengths that correspond with each weakness.

Negativity Bias

When you answered the questions in the last chapter, was it easier to identify your strengths or your weaknesses? Did you select more strengths or weaknesses? If you're like most people, you had an easier time identifying your weaknesses and you listed more weaknesses than strengths. This is because of a psychological phenomenon called the negativity bias.

Few people can see genius in someone who has offended them.

- Robertson Davies

Negativity bias means that we pay more attention to negative experiences and see them as more important and meaningful than positive experiences. In other words, we naturally notice our own weaknesses and have a more difficult time seeing or valuing our strengths.

Everyone has a negativity bias and that is why other people are more likely to criticize us for our weaknesses, instead of praising us for our strengths. Additionally, people tend to describe even our positive characteristics in a negative way. But we have to remember that their descriptions aren't correct. They are biased.

The Freak Factor

He has all the virtues I dislike and none of the vices I admire.

— Sir Winston Churchill

Fundamental Attribution Error

There is another reason that other people consistently, and incorrectly, see us as less than we truly are. It seems to be human nature to attribute negative motives and characteristics to others. Social psychologists call this fundamental attribution error.

Specifically, we tend to dismiss situational explanations for others' behavior and believe, instead, that something is inherently wrong with them. For example, if someone is acting nervous in an interview, we usually perceive that they are unqualified or have something to hide. The obvious explanation is that they are nervous because they are in an interview. The situation, not their personal characteristics, is likely the cause of their anxiety.

This almost unavoidable error is another reason why other people consistently focus on our weaknesses and fail to detect our strengths. Unfortunately we don't recognize this and begin to believe what other people tell us about ourselves.

The bottom-line is that most people don't know what they are talking about when they criticize us. Many of the problems that we have stem from the fact that we pay too much attention to what others think about us.

Nature never repeats herself, and the possibilities of one human soul will never be found in another.

— Elizabeth Cady Stanton

The author, George Eliot, is a great illustration of foolish perceptual errors. George was actually a woman. Her real name was Mary Ann Evans. She used a male pen name because, at that point in history, society didn't take female authors seriously. Her plan worked and to this day, schoolchildren throughout America are required to read her classic book, *Silas Marner.* This is just another example of how other people are inherently biased and inaccurate judges of character.

> Limitations and liabilities are the flip side of our gifts...
> a particular weakness is the inevitable trade-off for
> a particular strength.

— Parker Palmer, *Let Your Life Speak*

A Love and Hate Story

In order to move from awareness to acceptance, we have to discover the connection between our weaknesses and strengths.

Adventurous Al loves to take risks. He loves to explore and try new things. He loves to travel and rarely spends a lot of time in one place. His work experience includes a variety of short-term jobs that he works just long enough to finance his next trip. This means that he has few assets or material possessions. For example, he doesn't own a car or a house. He doesn't even rent an apartment. If he needs a place to sleep, he just stays at a friend's house or in a cheap motel. He's quick to try any sport that is new and danger-ous. He lives for the moment and has no plans for the future. During one of his trips, he meets a beautiful woman named Librarian Lucy.

Lucy loves stability and security. She carries a planner with a detailed list of things to do. Her goals are aligned with long-term objectives. Lucy's career is steadily moving forward. Even though she is still in her 20's, she has money in her retirement plan and has already purchased a home. Her wedding is already planned, despite the fact that she is not even dating, and she has even picked out the names of all her potential children. Lucy loves the routine and consistency of her life.

When Lucy and Al first met, they were instantly attracted to each other. We've all heard that opposites attract, but why does that happen? It seems like we are drawn to those characteristics that we don't have. We admire those qualities in the other person and wish we could be more like them. Al found Lucy attractive because she was everything he was not. Lucy found all attractive because he was everything that she was not.

Additionally, Lucy is everything that people have told Al that he should be. People are always telling him that he needs to settle down and grow up. Similarly, Al is everything that people have told Lucy that she should be. People are always telling her that she needs to loosen up and take it easy. They've been told their whole life that they should have the characteristics that the other person possesses. This is their chance to become better people.

So Al and Lucy got married and looked forward to a wonderful life together. Five years after their wedding, how are Al and Lucy doing? Do they still admire the other person's unique qualities? Are they still in love?

Unfortunately, the answer is no. They can't stand to be together and they are on the brink of divorce. How did this happen?

To answer that, consider two other questions. Has Lucy changed? No. Is Al a different person? Again, the answer is no.

Their love didn't die because they didn't get what they bargained for. Al is still adventurous. Lucy is still conservative. The difference is that they no longer see the other person in a positive light. They've taken the very characteristics that created the initial attraction and have turned them into negative qualities.

Lucy used to see Al as easy going, adventurous and spontaneous. Now she sees him as irresponsible, dangerous and impulsive.

Easy Going	became	Irresponsible
Adventurous	became	Dangerous
Spontaneous	became	Impulsive

Al used to see Lucy as structured, responsible and cautious. Now he sees her as rigid, controlling and fearful.

Structured	became	Rigid and Inflexible
Responsible	became	Controlling
Cautious	became	Fearful

These critical descriptions are simply the opposite of the very strengths that brought them together. Al and Lucy had hoped the other person's positive qualities would rub off on them; instead they ended up rubbing them the wrong way.

This is negativity bias at work. We tend to see the down side, the dark side, of other people's good qualities. The difficulty is that both descriptions are true. Al is irresponsible and easy going. Lucy is inflexible and structured. They are two sides of the same coin.

Since both descriptions are accurate, we can decide how we evaluate ourselves and others. Psychologists refer to this process of choosing our perspective as framing. For example, a beautiful frame can enhance the beauty of a painting but a broken, damaged or mismatched frame can detract from the attractiveness of the same painting. In the same way, the way we frame our characteristics, or those of others, can have a significant impact on how we think, feel and behave.

I believe that we look at ourselves in exactly the same way that Al and Lucy looked at each other. We frame our unique qualities in a negative way. We don't need to fix or remediate those qualities. That doesn't work. It's a waste of our energy, and it leads to unhappiness.

What we have to do is acknowledge that we aren't broken and we don't need to be fixed. In most cases there is nothing wrong, except for the way we look at ourselves. We need to learn to frame our uniqueness in a positive way.

To wish you were someone else is to waste the person you are.

- Friedrich Nietzsche

Reframing

In *Enemy of the State*, a conspiracy-theory thriller, Gene Hackman tries to help Will Smith evade government agents who are trying to capture him. Smith sees his situation as hopeless but Hackman changes his perspective by offering a lesson in guerrilla warfare. "You use your weakness as strength. They're big and you're small. But that means they're slow and you're fast. They're exposed and you're hidden." Notice how he reframes apparent strength (being big) as weakness (slow and exposed) and apparent weakness (being small) as strength (fast and hidden).

Like many people, I had strengths that were also flaws.

- Randy Pausch, *The Last Lecture*

Recently my dad saw a girl wearing a t-shirt that said, "I'm not bossy. I just know what you should be doing." I found another one that says, "I'm not bossy, I just have better ideas." Both of these messages reframe bossiness, an apparent weakness, as the possession of superior knowledge, an obvious strength.

It may seem like reframing is just denial, dishonesty or spin control. You might think that bossy people have a real problem and need to stop telling everyone what to do. That is why I love Erika's story, which shows that reframing can be the first step toward finding positive outlets for our seemingly negative traits.

The Freak Factor

Freak Profile: Erika Lyremark

Erika Lyremark is a coach, speaker, founder of DailyWhip.com, and author of *Think Like A Stripper: How To Hustle Your Business In Any Economy*. After spending nine years as an exotic dancer, Erika finally had enough and co-created a multimillion-dollar commercial real estate investment firm. With her passion and drive restored, she then realized that she had a deep desire to light a fire under the countless other souls out there toiling in a life that was not their own. I recently met Erika via Twitter, @DailyWhip, and was intrigued by her unconventional approach. I asked her if she had a freak factor story and her response is below.

"When I was a young girl, I got into trouble for being bossy. 'Erika, stop bossing your friends around. Erika, stop bossing your brother and sister around. Erika, stop bossing me around,' my mother would belt out in her thick Swedish accent.

Personally I never saw my bossiness as a problem. It got me a lot of things when I was younger. When my friends came over I got them to do my chores for me. I got the best Barbie doll at playtime. I got the best seat on the school bus. I got to be first in line.

Even though being bossy has gotten me into a lot of trouble and has been the cause of many fights with my friends and family, embracing my bossiness has been a huge advantage in my career. What was just a personality defect is now how I make my living.

Making change in one's life can be a grueling and ugly process that requires hardcore accountability. It is human nature that when we're confronted with facing the ugly truth about ourselves and our lives, we want to run as fast as we can back to our comfort zone. This is why my skill of artfully pushing, prodding, and 'whipping' my clients into action is key. Bossing my clients all the way to career success and life fulfillment has been a very effective approach."

Cheryl Cran at the *Brazen Careerist* blog reframes being a control freak as a positive attribute. She offers five reasons that it is good to be a control freak. They have self-discipline, get things done, take responsibility for their success, are decisive and provide direction and guidance. Cran ends with these words of encouragement. "If someone calls you a control freak, don't freak out. Instead… stand proud!" I couldn't have said it better myself.

George Will has even offered a positive spin on pessimism. "The nice part about being a pessimist is that you are constantly being either proven right or pleasantly surprised." He probably said this in an attempt at humor but his sarcastic comment is actually supported by research. Studies into happiness clearly demonstrate that low expectations lead to happiness. Denmark was found to be the happiest country in the world, not because of their weather, economy, or other positive circumstances, but because they have low expectations. When things go well, they are "pleasantly surprised."

Beyond the psychological benefits of pessimism, there are also career advantages to a negative outlook. Pessimists seem to make better lawyers than their more optimistic colleagues. This may be because their cynical view of life and human nature matches the reality of legal disputes. Divorces, lawsuits and criminal trials seem to bring out the worst in everyone, which is exactly what a pessimist would expect.

Every limit is a beginning as well as an ending.

- George Eliot

The truth is that there is nothing wrong with you. Each of us has unique characteristics. These neutral characteristics have both positive and negative features. These features, which we usually refer to as strengths and weaknesses, cannot be separated. They come in pairs. The positive and negative elements are inextricably linked. It's common to believe that there's nothing strong about your particular weaknesses. However, every weakness has a corresponding strength.

The great epochs of our life come when we gain the courage to rechristen our evil as what is best in us.

- Nietzsche, *Beyond Good and Evil*

Below is a chart of weaknesses and their corresponding strengths. Make a list of the top five strengths and weaknesses that you identified in the last chapter. Put a check mark next to each of them on the chart below. Are there any matches? Can you see how your weaknesses might be connected to your strengths?

Strength

1. Creative, Innovative
2. Organized, Systematic

3. Dedicated, Persistent
4. Flexible, Adaptable

5. Enthusiastic, Passionate
6. Calm, Laid-Back

7. Dynamic, Active
8. Reflective, Thoughtful

9. Adventurous, Courageous
10. Responsible, Cautious

11. Activist, Revolutionary
12. Conventional, Traditional

13. Direct, Honest
14. Polite, Courteous

15. Cooperative, Helpful
16. Competitive, Assertive

17. Theoretical, Idealistic
18. Realistic, Practical

19. Independent, Self-Sufficient
20. Team Player, Unselfish

21. Objective, Unbiased
22. Sensitive, Caring

23. Humble, Modest
24. Confident, Secure

25. Patient, Cautious
26. Spontaneous, Instinctive

Weakness

1. Chaotic, Disorganized
2. Rigid, Inflexible

3. Stubborn, Obstinate
4. Inconsistent, Unreliable

5. Quick-Tempered, Angry
6. Unfeeling, Emotionless

7. Frantic, Restless
8. Quiet, Shy

9. Reckless, Irresponsible
10. Boring, Uninteresting

11. Rebellious, Radical
12. Old-Fashioned, Conformist

13. Blunt, Rude
14. Superficial, Insincere

15. Passive, Submissive
16. Antagonistic, Aggressive

17. Unrealistic, Impractical
18. Negative, Critical

19. Isolated, Selfish
20. Dependent, Needy

21. Detached, Insensitive
22. Vulnerable, Emotional

23. Timid, Insecure
24. Arrogant, Conceited

25. Slow, Indecisive
26. Impatient, Impulsive

Strength	Weakness
27. Influential, Powerful	27. Controlling, Manipulative
28. Obedient, Dutiful	28. Weak, Subservient
29. Motivated, Ambitious	29. Obsessive, Workaholic
30. Relaxed, Easygoing	30. Unmotivated, Lazy
31. Analytical, Rational	31. Critical, Judgmental
32. Compassionate, Sympathetic	32. Lenient, Indulgent
33. Positive, Encouraging	33. Flattering, Naive
34. Realistic, Sensible	34. Negative, Discouraging
35. Open-Minded, Tolerant	35. Unprincipled, Naive
36. Certain, Decisive	36. Opinionated, Dogmatic
37. Extravagant, Elegant	37. Complicated, Difficult
38. Simple, Natural	38. Plain, Dull
39. Self-Controlled, Disciplined	39. Harsh, Stiff
40. Fun, Entertaining	40. Hedonistic, Self-Indulgent
41. Serious, Mature	41. Humorless, Solemn
42. Funny, Amusing	42. Silly, Immature
43. Focused	43. Limited, Restricted, Narrow
44. Exploring, Discovering	44. Distractible, Unfocused
45. Generous, Altruistic	45. Pushover, Sucker
46. Frugal, Thrifty	46. Stingy, Cheap
47. Curious, Inquisitive	47. Intrusive, Nosy
48. Content, Satisfied	48. Apathetic, Indifferent
49. Loyal, Devoted	49. Robotic, Gullible
50. Adaptable, Flexible	50. Disloyal, Fickle
51. Detail-Oriented, Meticulous	51. Perfectionist, Compulsive
52. Global, General	52. Sloppy, Careless

The Freak Factor

Strong people always have strong weaknesses too.
Where there are peaks, there are valleys.

- Peter Drucker

When I understand this liability as a trade-off for my strengths,
something new and liberating arises within me.

I no longer want to have my liability 'fixed.'

– Parker Palmer

The Myth of Perfection

Instead of seeing weaknesses as natural and unavoidable consequences of corresponding strengths, many people see weaknesses as problems to be eliminated. As I explained earlier, when I ask students and seminar participants if they should fix weaknesses, build strengths or do both, most choose to do both (fix weaknesses and build strengths). Similarly, the majority of respondents to The Freak Factor survey chose to fix weaknesses and become well-rounded.

- 52% agreed and only 35% disagreed with "If I want to improve, I need to fix my weaknesses."

- 52% agreed and only 33% disagreed with "It is important to be well-rounded, especially at work."

- 52% agreed and only 30% disagreed with "I should fix my weaknesses and build my strengths."

- 56% agreed and only 26% disagreed with "A well-balanced set of characteristics will make me more marketable."

2. acceptance

There are a number of problems with this approach. First, efforts to eliminate weaknesses are doomed to fail because, as I have shown, any characteristic can be considered a strength or a weakness.

Strengths	Weaknesses
1. Creative, Innovative	1. Chaotic, Disorganized
2. Organized, Systematic	2. Rigid, Inflexible

For example, consider the first strength/weakness combination in the chart (Creative vs. Organized). Creative people tend to be disorganized. Because they think "outside of the box," they tend to have difficulty putting things away in boxes. Fixing the weakness of disorganization doesn't make you better. It just makes you less creative and more organized.

Organized people tend to be inflexible because they want everything in the right box and they believe there is a box and a label that is color coded for everything. Fixing the weakness of inflexibility doesn't make you better. It just makes you less organized and more creative.

Fixing any weakness doesn't make you stronger. It just trades one weakness for another.

Strengths	Weaknesses
5. Enthusiastic, Passionate	5. Quick-Tempered, Angry
6. Calm, Laid-Back	6. Unfeeling, Emotionless

You might have noticed that the 52 strengths and weaknesses on the chart are divided into 26 pairs. Each strength in the pair is the opposite of the other. For example, (1) Creative is the opposite of (2) Organized. (5) Enthusiastic is the opposite of (6) Calm, etc. It isn't possible to be more enthusiastic and calmer. Becoming more enthusiastic requires you to become less calm.

The Freak Factor

I've tried to illustrate this visually below. As you maximize your score on enthusiasm (10), it minimizes your score on calmness (0). As you maximize your score on calmness (10), it minimizes your score on enthusiasm (0). Attempting to have a little of both just leaves you with a mediocre score on both enthusiasm (5) and calmness (5). Because they are opposites, you can't increase them both at the same time.

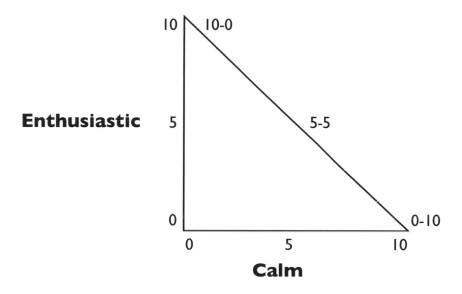

Because of this relationship between strengths and weaknesses, the best approach is maximize whichever strength/weakness combination that you already have, since this is your natural style, at the expense of the opposing combination. For example, one of my strengths is that I'm enthusiastic and passionate, which means that one of my weaknesses is that I can be quick-tempered and angry. If I focus my efforts on being less angry, it will decrease my enthusiasm. I'll become calmer but will then have the related weakness of being emotionless. The likely result is that I'll just become neither enthusiastic nor calm.

Patient, Cautious	Slow, Indecisive
Spontaneous, Instinctive	Impatient, Impulsive

Good things may come to those who wait…
but only the things left by those who hustle.

- Abraham Lincoln

This quote from Lincoln shows that, although patience is a virtue, it isn't without its limitations. Patience can also be slowness and indecisiveness. Impatience, an apparent weakness, can also be beneficial, when it causes us to move quickly and create new opportunities. Since every weakness has a corresponding strength, replacing a weakness with a strength just adds a different weakness.

Independent, Self-Sufficient	Isolated, Selfish
Team Player, Unselfish	Dependent, Needy

Like I always say, there's no 'I' in 'team'.
There is a 'me', though, if you jumble it up.

- David Shore

Cooperation is certainly beneficial and many people are good team players. However, independence is also a positive characteristic and strong individual performers don't always play well with the other boys and girls. As Michael Jordan explained, "there's no 'I' in 'team,' but there is an 'I' in 'win.'"

When you choose anything, you reject everything else…
so when you take one course of action you
give up all the other courses.

– G.K. Chesterton

The second reason that fixing weaknesses doesn't work is that we have limited resources. Most people have too much to do and not enough time or energy to do it. It requires more time and energy to try to do both, instead of focusing exclusively on building strengths. I'll talk about the limits of self-control later in this chapter.

The Freak Factor

Third, focusing on both activities limits progress. We end up with the worst of both worlds, expending a lot of effort without achieving the desired results. Fourth, doing both prevents us from becoming exceptional in any one area.

As Seth Godin explains in a recent blog post, a company that focuses exclusively in one area will almost always defeat a competitor that is trying to do a lot of things well. "When you have someone who is willing to accomplish A without worrying about B and C, they will almost always defeat you in accomplishing A… The single-minded have a fantastic advantage. And sometimes, their single-minded focus on accomplishing just that one thing (whatever it is) pushes them through the Dip far ahead of you and then yes, they make a ton of money and you've lost forever."

The same principle applies to individuals. While you are busy diffusing your time and energy broadly in an effort to improve in a variety of different areas, someone else is obsessively developing their strengths and flaunting their weaknesses. They aren't allowing their weaknesses to distract them from focusing on the areas in which they have the greatest potential. If you want to win, in your career or your business, you need to be single-minded. Don't let your weaknesses and the goal of being well-rounded keep you from a maniacal focus on improving your strengths.

Finally, and most importantly, since weaknesses and strengths are linked, attempting to fix a weakness can actually diminish the corresponding strength. To illustrate this process at work, let's take a look at the discount retail industry.

> If you think a weakness can be turned into a strength,
> I hate to tell you this, but that's another weakness.
>
> – Jack Handey, *Deep Thoughts*

The Kmart Fallacy

Wal-Mart's main strength is low prices, but its weaknesses include poor quality merchandise, long lines and unhelpful employees. Target's main strengths are higher quality products from well-known designers, attractive stores and helpful associates who are quick to open a new checkout lane. Unfortunately, Target's weakness is that its prices are not as low as those at Wal-Mart.

What would happen if Wal-Mart tried to fix their weaknesses? What would happen to their low prices, their primary strength, as they added better products and extra employees at the registers? The answer is simple. Their prices would climb, thus diminishing their strength.

What if Target decided to fix their weakness by lowering prices? What would happen to the level of customer service and the great products, which give them their advantage, if they focused more on cost cutting? Again, the answer is straightforward. Their quality and service would decrease, thus diminishing their strength.

For proof of this, just look at Kmart. They provide an illustration of what happens when a company, or individual, loses focus and tries to fix weaknesses, instead of focusing on strengths. Their historical leadership in discount retail was based on the blue-light special, a symbol of low prices. However, they did not focus exclusively on this price advantage and began to lose customers to Wal-Mart.

Kmart then began adding designer products from celebrities like Martha Stewart but wasn't quite ready to shed their low-price image. This allowed Target to capture higher-income customers that were design conscious, while Wal-Mart attracted lower-income customers who were cost-conscious.

Kmart's efforts to fix their weaknesses ultimately led to bankruptcy. They weren't the best at anything, so customers had no reason to shop there. Their failure illustrates the dangers of trying to eliminate weaknesses and be more well-rounded.

There is a compelling reason to go to Wal-Mart, low prices. There is a compelling reason to go to Target, better service and design. But there is no compelling reason to go to Kmart. Their prices aren't the lowest and their service and design aren't the best. They are just mediocre in both areas, so people don't shop there.

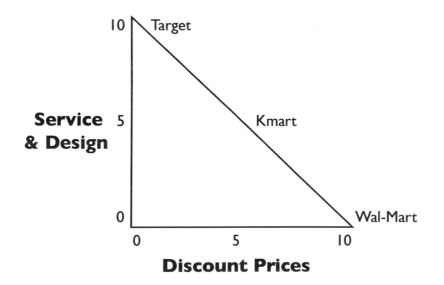

The Freak Factor

> It's so easy to try to compromise, to do both, to fit in AND stand out. There lies failure.
>
> **- Seth Godin, *Linchpin***

What is true for these companies is also true for individuals. When we try to fix our weaknesses, we end up damaging the corresponding strengths. Our efforts to make ourselves better end up making us worse. This is why it is so important to accept our weaknesses instead of trying to fix them.

Famous Freak: John Grisham

John Grisham is one of the most successful authors of the last twenty years. Starting with *The Firm*, his legal thrillers have been read by millions and then seen by millions more after being made into feature films. If effectiveness requires us to be well-rounded and balanced, then you'd expect to find those characteristics in the lives of exceptional people, like Grisham. But you don't.

Grisham has obvious weaknesses. But he's not trying to fix them. He accepts them and refuses to change. In the Author's Note section of Grisham's most recent book, *The Confession*, he writes: "Some overly observant readers may stumble across a fact or two that might appear to be in error. They may consider writing letters to point out my short-comings. They should conserve paper. There are mistakes in this book, as always, and as long as I continue to loathe research, while at the same time remaining perfectly content to occasionally dress up the facts, I'm afraid the mistakes will continue. My hope is that the errors are insignificant in nature."

What can we learn from Grisham's example?

- Grisham isn't listening to the criticism.
  (conserve paper)

- He admits the flaws.
  (there are mistakes)

- He explains that he is the source of the flaws.
  (loathing research, content to dress up facts)

- He refuses to change, to fix the flaws.
  (mistakes will continue)

- He reminds us that the flaws don't matter that much.
  (the errors are insignificant)

Curing or Crippling?

Earlier this year I was watching the new TV show, *Mental*. It follows the story of Jack Gallagher, a director at a psychiatric clinic. Jack caught my attention in the first episode when he stripped naked to help a delusional patient. Later in the show, he discovers that the patient, Vincent, used to be a talented artist. Unfortunately, the medication that supposedly fixed his mental illness also destroyed his creative abilities. The pills made Vincent normal and helped him to be a good employee in a warehouse, but took away his true talents.

The following conversation takes place in a meeting to discuss treatment for Vincent in which Jack argues for taking him off of the medication.

Carl: The pharmacology has been successful for a dozen years. Why deviate?

Jack: You call it a success. I say the patient has been crippled.

Nora: You mean creatively?

Jack: He was a gifted artist and for the last 12 years he's been stuck in a plumbing warehouse, moving boxes from one pile to another and that's about to get worse. He's about to get filed away in an institution for life.

Later in the show, Jack is talking with Vincent after he's stopped taking the medication.

Jack: How are you feeling?

Patient: I'm feeling. Everything seems really different.

Jack: The medication didn't just take away your ability to paint; it also took away the passions, the pains, the highs, the lows, everything that made you human.

Even if it is possible to repair, or even eliminate, our weaknesses, what will it cost? What talents are we destroying in the process of fixing our apparent shortcomings? Make sure you are ready to pay the price before you start renovating your life.

We are so accustomed to disguise ourselves to others that,
in the end, we become disguised to ourselves.

- Francois de La Rochefoucauld

The Myth of Unlimited Potential

But can't we change? This is a common question that I hear after sharing the Freak Factor with people. My answer to that is I believe that people don't change that much. For example, my grandparents are 90 years old and have been married for almost 70 years. My grandmother recently complained that my grandfather wasn't talking to her enough. He hasn't been talkative for the last 70 years and yet my grandmother is still hopeful that he's about to change. They've been arguing about this for nearly three quarters of a century and she still hasn't been able to accept that she married an introverted man, who doesn't have a lot to say.

In college I studied psychology and later earned a graduate degree in counseling psychology. Unfortunately, during my coursework I discovered that counseling required two skills that I didn't have, sitting still and listening; so much for that. It is important to note that, during my time in school, I received extensive training in empathy, listening, collaboration, group process and non-verbal communication, personality and behavior change. Despite this knowledge, I couldn't seem to change my behavior or transform my personality. I wasn't any better at sitting still, listening or doing what I was told. I tried to change. I wanted to change. I put years of effort into changing, but it didn't work.

Penelope Trunk, author of *The Brazen Careerist,* shares my belief in limited change. "Nothing changes when you grow up… I think I could have figured out right decisions for me a lot faster if I had realized how much we reveal about our true selves when we're young." Two things she learned about her younger self included apparent weaknesses. She had no patience for group learning and was a risk taker. That didn't change as she grew up and it still defines her work.

An article in the New York Times entitled *Can You Become a Creature of New Habits?* explains the science behind our inability to change. We are born with the ability to deal with challenges in a variety of ways, but during puberty "the brain shuts down half of that capacity, preserving only those modes of thought that have seemed most valuable during the first decade or so of life… This breaks the major rule in the American belief system — that anyone can do anything. That's a lie that we have perpetuated, and it fosters mediocrity. Knowing what you're good at and doing even more of it creates excellence."

We can change. We can improve. We can grow. However, our growth and development efforts should build on existing strengths, not attempt to overcome weaknesses.

Apparently, the brain is designed to build on past patterns of success, not to create completely new ones.

Robert Kurson's book, *Crashing Through*, tells the story of Mike May, a man who lost his sight at the age of three. Because of advances in medical science, Mike was able to regain partial sight as an adult. Unfortunately, his brain was no longer able to process visual information. The brain neurons that were usually dedicated to vision had been re-assigned to focus on non-vision related tasks. Despite being able to physically see images, Mike was never able to recognize faces or even differentiate between men and women. After years of blindness, it just wasn't possible for him to learn to see again.

You can't put feathers on a dog and call it a chicken.

– Dr. Phil McGraw

After being mauled by one of their tigers, the famous duo of Siegfried and Roy learned that you can't reliably change wild tigers into house cats. Similarly, after a killer whale drowned a trainer at Sea World, the park instituted a new policy forbidding trainers from being in the water with the whales. Killer whales and tigers will always be dangerous animals, regardless of efforts to tame them.

This same principle is true for people. We can't change our fundamental natures. Attempts to do so are slow, painful, frustrating and, ultimately, ineffective. Even if modest improvements are made, there isn't much of a payoff. Unfortunately, we've been taught that we can be whatever we want to be and that, with enough self control, we can do anything.

The Myth of Self-Control

What do you want? Do you want to be more organized, lose weight, get a promotion or have a better marriage? Most self-help books have one primary suggestion on how to do this: use self-discipline to simply act differently. They argue that if we just wanted it bad enough, we'd be able to make the change. In this view, people succeed because they have self-control and others fail because they lack self-control. I disagree.

There are three parts to the myth of self-control. First, we believe that people have unlimited potential. We are taught that we can do anything, if we are just willing to try hard enough. Therefore, if we aren't successful, it is not because of a lack of ability, it is because of a lack of effort. The second belief is directly tied to the first. We believe that self-discipline is the route to success. If we just had more self-control, we could achieve our goals. Third, we believe that success is the result of perseverance. If we just tried hard

The Freak Factor

enough and long enough, if we could stick with it over time and never give up, then we could succeed.

The truth is that everyone has the same amount of self-control. The key to success is determining how you will use the self-control that you have. In other words, you don't need more fuel; you just need to become more fuel efficient. I believe that we all have the same amount of self-control. We don't get more or less than anyone else. Successful people do not have extra discipline. They just use what they have more wisely.

Discipline and concentration are a matter of being interested.

– Tom Kite

In the June 2007 edition of Men's Health magazine, a University of Minnesota researcher explained that "dieting can increase the likelihood that you'll spend your money impulsively. Why? The scientists theorize that you have only a limited number of mental resources to allocate toward self-control. If you're using these resources to resist certain food cravings, you become more prone to giving in to other temptations."

As Roy Baumeister at Florida State University's Center for the Advancement of Health explains, "self-control comes in limited quantities and must be replenished." It is more like a renewable energy source than a learned skill. After individuals completed tasks requiring self-control, they had "less physical stamina and impulse control." Baumeister's experiments showed that "resisting temptation consumed an important resource (self-control), which was then less available to help the person persist in the face of failure."

Similarly, during her *Happiness Project*, Gretchen Rubin discovered that "relying on will power is very hard–so whenever possible, I abandon it.… Because self-control is a precious resource, try to use it as little as possible. Look for ways to engineer situations so they don't test your will power at all."

It's very difficult to motivate yourself to do something.
It's much easier to leverage what you are already
motivated to do.

- **Chris Guillebeau,** *The Art of Non-Conformity*

We often have difficulty because we are using our discipline in the wrong places, like trying to fix our weaknesses and trying to fit in by being someone we're not. These activities drain our energy. They sap our self-discipline. I met Kelly Rogers, a graduate student from Charlotte, NC, at Pam Slim's *Escape from Cubicle Nation* seminar last year. She put it this way. "Being who you are not is exhausting."

Pam Slim reminds us that "When you force yourself to do something you don't want to do, you have to deplete the energy from your body to do it. When you make it through a week where you have forced yourself to do work you don't enjoy, you will feel exhausted, drained, and in need of martinis, industrial-strength aspirin, and/or face-planted-in-pillow rest."

People think I'm disciplined.
It's not discipline, it is devotion.
There is a great difference.

– **Luciano Pavarotti**

How can we use our energy more efficiently? How can we get more out of our limited supply of self-control? We need to build on strengths, instead of trying to fix weaknesses. We need to develop our positive characteristics, instead of trying to change our natural preferences. These activities are fueled by devotion, not discipline. They rely on passion instead of pain. As Pam Slim explains, "When you do things you love, your body generates energy naturally. You may work an equal number of hours, or more, than when doing work you don't enjoy, but the difference is you will feel spent, not depleted."

Devotion is a great substitute for discipline. Discipline is scarce, but devotion is abundant. Discipline is painful, but devotion is enjoyable. Both act as fuel for our activities and we can choose which one we will use. It takes tremendous discipline to fix our weaknesses but devotion provides the energy for building on our strengths. As the world continues to search for alternative fuels to power our vehicles, maybe it is time to consider an alternative fuel for powering our lives. Devotion is more powerful and more abundant than discipline.

The Freak Factor

Preserving the Tilt

In 1173, the people who built the Leaning Tower of Pisa had some trouble creating a stable foundation. It started tipping over before they'd even finished building it. The builders tried to fix it but couldn't get it to straighten up. That was a very lucky break for the city of Pisa.

Millions of people have spent millions of dollars to visit the city for one reason, to see a tower that leans. The problem those builders were trying to fix is the very reason that so many people travel to this otherwise obscure location. As one of the many websites devoted to the tower explains, "because of its inclination, and its beauty, from 1173 up to the present the Tower has been the object of very special attention."

Even so, some people just can't handle a broken tower. In 1934, Benito Mussolini declared that the tower should be straightened. Fortunately, the effort to fix the tower failed and actually caused it to lean even more.

In 1964, the Italian government took steps to keep the tower from falling down. However, this time they decided it was "important to keep the current tilt, due to the vital role that this element played in promoting the tourism industry of Pisa."

There are four important lessons we can learn from this leaning tower. First, people go to see the tower because of its obvious flaw, not in spite of that flaw. Its weakness is its strength. The Tower's flaw is "vital" and has made it the "object of very special attention." We'll talk more about this idea in the next chapter on appreciation. Second, fixing the flaw would destroy the tower's uniqueness, but that didn't keep people from trying. Third, efforts to fix flaws usually fail. Fourth, it is worth the effort to maintain the flaw, to preserve the inclination, "to keep the current tilt." We'll talk about this more in the chapter on amplification.

Other people will always try to get you to straighten up. They will frame your strengths as weaknesses and demand that you fix them. Don't pay attention to them. Just keep leaning.

By the way, some people argue that the tilt was not an accident; it was intentional. If that is true, it is even better. The architect must have understood the tremendous power of uniqueness. How many other buildings have been so famous for so long?

2. acceptance

Reflect

- What drains you?

- Where are you currently burning a lot of fuel?

- Which activities are truly unavoidable?

- How could you alternate these with tasks that renew your energy?

- What renews you energy?

- How can you improve your fuel efficiency?

- Create a list of activities that seem effortless or that leave you feeling energized.

- Think of situations where you lose track of time.

- How could you spend more time doing these activities?

- Review the relationships between your strengths and weaknesses.

- Can you see how working to fix a weakness could actually diminish one your strengths?

- Consider situations in which you are currently trying to fix a weakness and build a strength.

- What would happen if you focused exclusively on building the strength?

- How could that help you to become exceptional?

The Freak Factor

3. appreciation

we succeed because of our weaknesses, not in spite of them

White collar conservative flashin' down the street, pointing that plastic finger at me. They all assume my kind will drop and die, but I'm gonna wave my freak flag high.

— Jimi Hendrix

As we saw in the last chapter, each of our weaknesses has a corresponding strength. Because of this, we need to reframe our unique characteristics in a positive, instead of negative, way. We need to wave our freak flags high.

The following stories show how seemingly obvious weaknesses actually conceal surprising strengths. These examples illustrate the unique relationship between strengths and weaknesses. It is my hope that they will move you from simply accepting your weaknesses to intense appreciation for your apparent flaws.

Our strength grows out of our weakness.

- Ralph Waldo Emerson, *Compensation*

Disorganization

It's good to be neat and it's bad to be messy. At least that's what we're told. We've all heard that "cleanliness is next to godliness" and "a cluttered desk is a sign of a cluttered mind." Furthermore, most people believe that they would be happier and more successful if they were more organized. This desire is evidenced by the success of the Container Store and the endless list of television shows dedicated to cleaning up and reorganizing messy homes. Being disorganized seems like an obvious weakness. People who can't get organized have a flaw that they need to fix. Don't they?

Not necessarily. In *A Perfect Mess: The Hidden Benefits of Disorder*, David Freedman and Eric Abrahamson argue that messiness is actually a strength and should be "celebrated rather than avoided." They provide evidence that there are significant benefits to disorder. Andy Rooney, the quirky commentator for 60 Minutes, agrees saying, "creativity doesn't come out of order; it comes out of messiness."

Additionally, Alexander Fleming discovered penicillin while sorting through his cluttered lab after returning from a long vacation. If his lab had been clean and organized, we might not have access to life saving antibiotics. Albert Einstein, probably one of the most creative minds of the 20th century, challenged the enemies of clutter by asking, "If a cluttered desk is a sign of a cluttered mind, then what is an empty desk a sign of?"

In this case, the seeming weakness of disorganization is offset by the strength of creativity. However, disorganization could be considered a personality trait or behavioral preference. What about actual disabilities?

> Rough diamonds may sometimes be mistaken
> for worthless pebbles.
>
> - Sir Thomas Browne

Dyslexia

Dyslexia is a disability. People with dyslexia get letters and words mixed up and this leads to major problems with reading and writing. This, in turn, is a major barrier to success. Or is it?

A recent study showed that 35% of small business owners have dyslexia. This is significant because only one-tenth of Americans have dyslexia, but they make up more than one-third of entrepreneurs in the US. Another study found that people with dyslexia are far more likely to become millionaires. In fact, almost half of the millionaires in the sample had dyslexia.

A well-known person who appreciates his weaknesses is Richard Branson, billionaire and founder of the Virgin companies. When asked if his dyslexia has hindered his business success, Branson said "strangely, I think my dyslexia has helped." Other famous individuals who've lived with learning disabilities include: John Chambers, CEO of Cisco, Ingvar Kamprad, founder of IKEA, and Charles Schwab, founder of the discount brokerage firm that bears his name.

What explains this apparent relationship between disability and success? Researchers believe that "most people who make a million have difficult childhoods or have been frustrated in a major way. Dyslexia is one of the driving forces behind that." Having dyslexia makes the person a freak and leaves them "outside of the mainstream social groups in school."

However, it seems that dyslexia is a two-edged sword. The obvious weaknesses and problems are accompanied by important strengths. Experts suggest that people with dyslexia are often better than most at being "creative and looking at the bigger picture" and this can make them better strategic thinkers. Daniel Pink, author of *A Whole New Mind*, believes that some of these advantages might result from a greater ability to use the right side of the brain. Others suggest that "individuals who have difficulty reading and writing tend to deploy other strengths." They don't focus on their disability. Instead, they focus on their unique abilities.

I recently read *Your Child's Strengths* by Jenifer Fox. In discussing learning disabilities like dyslexia, Fox writes, "perhaps there is not something wrong with people who process differently. Maybe it is not a weakness at all. Maybe it is a clue to what might be fertile ground for the sprouting of a great strength." She goes on to support her argument by explaining that many children with learning disabilities are also labeled as "gifted and talented."

Unfortunately, when we do things differently, we are often criticized and given negative labels. As Kelly, a participant at a recent conference, explained "I think with my mouth open." This did not make her popular with her teachers. Shaun Cassidy, a local artist, had a similar experience. "I think with my hands, not my brains." He struggled to learn in traditional contexts and didn't find success until he was able to deploy his unique learning style as an artist.

Famous Freak: Paul Orfalea

One example of a dyslexic millionaire was Paul, who grew up in a hard-working middle-class family in Southern California. In second grade, he still didn't know the alphabet. Efforts by his teachers, parents and siblings didn't seem to help. He was eventually diagnosed with both dyslexia and ADHD. After failing a few grades and being expelled from several schools, he finally graduated from high school with a 1.2 grade point average and a ranking of 1,482 out of 1,500 students. His only surprise was that anyone did worse than he did.

Based on his disability and poor performance in school, most people wouldn't have predicted success for Paul. In fact, Paul himself was often concerned that he would end up homeless. He started a small business selling school supplies and copies in a store so small that he had to move the copier out to the sidewalk. The business eventually grew to 1200 locations in 10 different countries and, in 2004, Paul Orfalea sold Kinko's to FedEx for more than $2 billion.

How did a dyslexic guy who can't read or write build such a successful business? Orfalea argues that he succeeded because of his disability, not in spite of it. Because of his weaknesses, he had to trust others and rely on them to help him run the business. For example, he needed people to assist him with correspondence. This evolved into a culture of teamwork and collaboration that separated Kinko's from their competitors.

Because he was restless, he spent most of his time out of his office and in the stores, observing the practices of frontline employees. Because he was impulsive, he quickly implemented new ideas throughout the organization. His intuitive intelligence and racing mind made him impatient and easily frustrated, but many employees credit these traits with creating a sense of urgency that motivated people to make changes and improvements.

These positive elements of Orfalea's dyslexia are confirmed by Sally Shaywitz, a professor at the Yale University School of Medicine. Her research indicates that people with dyslexia have an exceptional talent for creative thinking. Additionally, hyperactivity is often a driver for action and contributes to an adventurous spirit that leads entrepreneurs to take chances that others might consider too risky.

Orfalea wrote *Copy This! Lessons from a Hyperactive Dyslexic who Turned a Bright Idea into One of America's Best Companies* with journalist Ann Marsh, but because of his dyslexia, he's never been able to read his own book. In it, he credits his disabilities for his success and says he thinks everyone should have dyslexia and ADHD. During his many speaking engagements, he advises audiences to "like yourself, not despite your flaws and so-called deficits, but because of them." He definitely appreciates his weaknesses and understands how they correspond to his many positive qualities.

Disorganization and dyslexia both illustrate the dual nature of certain characteristics but what about destructive behaviors that are truly harmful, like addiction?

My life is not only about my strengths and virtues;
it is also about my liabilities and my limits,
my trespasses and my shadow…

We must embrace what we dislike or find shameful about
ourselves as well as what we are confident and proud of.

– Parker Palmer

The Freak Factor

Addiction

Todd Crandell had been a drug addict for almost 15 years. He was homeless, destitute, afraid and alone. He had lost everything that mattered to him. But in 2007, he founded a successful nonprofit organization and the author of a bestselling book *Racing for Recovery: From Addict to Ironman*. He has completed numerous Ironman triathlons (2.4 mile swim, 112 mile bike, 26.2 mile run) and has a loving wife and four children.

How did he do it? How did he transform his life? He harnessed his addiction. Todd hasn't really stopped being an addict. He's just addicted to something new, Ironman triathlons.

His former coach put it this way: "He's changed his addiction to a positive addiction and he's now used it as a platform to help others. And so, he has no choice, his body's going to have to fall apart before he'll stop."

Crandell is still abusing his body. He's still obsessed. He's still addicted. ESPN SportsCenter reporter, Tom Rinaldi, put it this way, "he found his new focus in a passion as extreme as his addiction, the grueling pursuit of a triathlon."

> What if there were addictions that, instead of making you weaker, made you stronger?

> **- William Glasser, psychologist and author of *Positive Addiction***

Todd's weakness was his intensity, but it was also his strength. In an interview, Crandell said, "The same tenacity I put into destroying myself, I just needed to switch it and put it into repairing myself." Crandell isn't a new person. He hasn't undergone a fundamental change in personality. He has just discovered and applied the positive aspects of his unique personality.

So it isn't surprising that he didn't stop with just one new addiction. He also founded Racing for Recovery, a nonprofit organization that helps addicts find hope and health through athletic pursuit. However, "providing that hope became Crandell's new addiction, but like his old one, it's come with great financial and emotional cost."

He lost everything again. He had cars repossessed and houses foreclosed and that is after becoming sober. His financial losses were due to his fanatical pursuit of the organization's mission and he made no apologies. "How can you look at who I was and who I am today and not say 'this is what I'm supposed to do'?" Crandell can't do anything just a little. He can't take it easy. He can't slow down.

His strength is his weakness. The two are inseparable. His pursuit of the Ironman is "an addiction, perhaps, but also a mission and a purpose - to keep making the journey from addict to inspiration."

Insanity

The ancient philosopher, Seneca, said that "there is no great genius without a touch of madness." In his mind, genius and insanity aren't two separate conditions; they are both part of the same condition. If you have one, you have the other.

Apple celebrates the connection between genius and madness in their Think Different commercial. "Here's to the crazy ones, the misfits, the rebels, the troublemakers, the round pegs in the square holes, the ones who see things differently. They're not fond of rules and they have no respect for the status quo. You can quote them, disagree with them, glorify or vilify them. About the only thing you can't do is ignore them. Because they change things. They push the human race forward. And while some may see them as the crazy ones, we see genius. Because the people who are crazy enough to think they can change the world are the ones who do. Think Different."

Unfortunately, not everyone appreciates people who are different. A few months after my friend's son, Jim, started kindergarten, the teacher diagnosed him as having attention deficit hyperactivity disorder and oppositional defiant disorder, which is defined as a pattern of angry, hostile and disobedient behavior. Naturally, my friends were concerned about their son and had him evaluated by a psychologist. The tests showed that he had an IQ in the genius range. He didn't have a problem. He had a gift that looked like a problem.

I think this happens more than we think. Every day bosses, teachers, spouses, co-workers and friends misdiagnose genius as madness. Sometimes we even do it to ourselves. Once this happens, the attempts at healing begin. Unfortunately, healing the madness can destroy the genius.

Kay Redfield Jamison, Ph.D., a professor of psychiatry at the Johns Hopkins University School of Medicine also supports Seneca's argument. She wrote a fascinating book, *Touched With Fire: Manic-Depressive Illness and the Artistic Temperament*, which suggests that mental illness might actually be a requirement for creating great art.

Jamison argues that "most artistic geniuses were (and are) manic depressives" and that "psychological suffering is an essential component of artistic creativity." This might seem like a wild proposition. So it is also important to note that Kay is a scientist and has researched this connection extensively. She also has manic-depression.

The most astonishing response to Jamison's book comes from Robert Bernard Martin, Professor Emeritus at Princeton University. "By the end of the book the reader has been

The Freak Factor

quietly rerouted to the profoundly ethical question of whether the eradication of this disease (manic-depression) by modern molecular biology would not ultimately be a diminution of the human race."

That is a strong statement. Martin is implying that curing manic-depression could diminish people's ability to create fine art. If this is true, then fostering this condition might increase people's creative impulses.

Similarly, Michael Maccoby, author of *The Productive Narcissist: The Promise and Peril of Visionary Leadership,* believes that the negative characteristics of narcissistic leaders, extreme sensitivity to criticism, unwillingness to listen, paranoia, extreme competitiveness, anger, exaggeration, isolation and grandiosity are inextricably tied to their positive characteristics, independent thinking, passion, charisma, voracious learning, perseverance, sense of humor, risk-taking and desire to change the world. His research shows that it isn't possible to benefit from the advantages of the narcissistic personality without suffering from the disadvantages. They are inextricably linked.

I used to see Tourette's as a curse, but now I consider it a blessing. It's made me who I am.

- **Dave Pittman,** *American Idol* contestant

Amputation

Oscar Pistorius is fast. And because he is one of the fastest men in the world for 400 meters, he wanted to go to the Olympics. Unfortunately, the IAAF wasn't going to let him. They thought he had an unfair advantage.

Was he taking steroids or human growth hormone? No. Was he doping his blood? No. His unfair advantage is that he is a double-amputee. He was born without a fibula in either of his legs. As a child, both of his legs were amputated below the knee.

His prosthetic legs, called Cheetahs, are custom-designed carbon fiber blades. These artificial legs are the supposed source of his unfair advantage and the source of the controversy surrounding his efforts to make the South African Olympic team.

Ross Tucker, PH.D. offered this assessment in the April 2008 edition of Runner's World. "While it's impossible to determine exactly how much time the physiological differences save Pistorius in a 400-meter race, it's clear we're talking about seconds rather than milliseconds."

3. appreciation

In other words, Pistorius is actually faster without normal legs than he would be with them. His disability gives him a super-ability. His apparent weakness is a strength.

Specifically, his artificial legs give him the following advantages over normal runners:

- Less energy loss
- Superior energy return
- Equal speed with less energy
- Less vertical motion
- Less fatigue (if you don't have legs, they can't get tired)

It was a rollercoaster ride for Pistorius. After the IAAF ruled that he could not compete in the Olympics, their decision was overruled by the Court of Arbitration. Unfortunately, Pistorius then failed to qualify for the Olympic team by less than one second. He will try again in 2012. Meanwhile, he plans to dominate the Paralympic Games, as long as they don't ban him for not being disabled enough.

Another paralympian, Tatanya McFadden, proudly declares, "I see my disability as an ability." Her perspective shows that things are not always what they seem and that the line between strength and weakness may not be as clear as we think.

Conviction

Catherine Rohr is the founder of the Prison Entrepreneurship Program (PEP). The mission of PEP is to provide inmates with the equivalent of a MBA degree. Rohr believes that prisoners can succeed after their release if they have the right tools. PEP provides them with the support and education that they need to build a legitimate business.

Rohr is a former Wall Street investor who toured a prison and "noticed that executives and inmates had more in common than most would think. They know how to manage others to get things done. Even the most unsophisticated drug dealers inherently understand business concepts such as competition, profitability, risk management and proprietary sales channels. For both executives and inmates, passion is instinctive."

After having this realization, she made it her goal to help inmates to develop and operate legitimate businesses. She believed that it was possible to channel the "entrepreneurial passions and influential personalities of the inmates–intentionally recruiting former gang leaders, drug dealers and hustlers."

Her initial business plan competition combined the efforts of 55 inmates and 15 senior executives and was an unqualified success. In a live interview with Catherine at the Catalyst Conference in Atlanta she described the inmates this way. "These men are already proven entrepreneurs." She then explained that many of the PEP graduates go on to earn legitimate six-figure incomes. This drew a collective jealous groan from many of the poorly compensated ministry leaders and nonprofit managers in the audience.

Catherine's program is a phenomenal example of the power of finding strength inside apparent weakness and framing seemingly negative characteristics in a positive way. If Rohr can do this with convicted felons, what could we accomplish with our less severe flaws?

Famous Freak: Randy Pausch

Randy Pausch, Carnegie Mellon professor, husband, and father of three young children, died of pancreatic cancer in July 2008. The video of his *Last Lecture* has been viewed more than five million times on YouTube and *The Last Lecture* book was a bestseller. I recently read the book and was inspired and deeply moved by his story.

In the book, Pausch describes himself as arrogant, tactless, blunt, a know-it-all, an efficiency freak and "a tough teacher with high expectations and some quirky ways… I'm a bit of an acquired taste… I had strengths that were also flaws." His good friend Scott Sherman described Pausch as a person who completely lacked tact and was likely to offend nearly anyone that he met. These unique characteristics, which some might see as weaknesses, are the primary reasons that he was recently named one of the Top 100 Most Influential People in the World by *Time* magazine.

After his wife, Jai, accidentally crashed one of their cars into their other car, Pausch didn't get upset. This surprised Jai, who was afraid that he would be angry with her. She was even more surprised, and upset, when he explained that he wasn't even going to get the cars fixed, since it was just body damage. Then he explained, "'You can't have just some of me, Jai,' I told her. 'You appreciate the part of me that didn't get angry because two things we own got hurt. But the flip side of that is my belief that you don't repair things if they still do what they are supposed to do.'"

Not everything needs to be fixed. Our weaknesses don't need to be fixed because they are linked to our strengths. But there is another reason to appreciate our weaknesses. It turns out that limitations can be very helpful.

> We have to know 'the necessary limitations of our nature beyond which we cannot trespass with impunity.'
>
> - W.H. Auden

Limitation

We need to appreciate our weaknesses, instead of just accepting them, because seemingly restrictive limitations can actually help us succeed. Shaun Cassidy is an artist in residence at the McColl Center for Visual Art in Charlotte, North Carolina. He led a one-hour creativity exercise during a workshop that I attended recently. During the activity he argued that "seemingly negative parameters can actually help you to be more innovative."

Cassidy's perspective is supported by significant evidence. Social theorist, Barry Schwartz, in his book, *The Paradox of Choice*, explains that when we have too many choices, we struggle to make decisions. He encourages us to "learn to love constraints" because "as the number of choices we face increases, freedom of choice becomes a tyranny of choice. Routine decisions take so much time and attention that it becomes difficult to get through the day. In circumstances like this, we should learn to view limits on the possibilities that we face as liberating not constraining."

Ironically, more options don't liberate us, they paralyze us. As Erich Fromm explained in *Escape from Freedom*, "people are beset not by a lack of opportunity but by a dizzying abundance of it." It is counter-intuitive, but limitations, not options, are what liberate us.

Similarly, behavioral economist, Dan Ariely, in *Predictably Irrational,* argues that the common strategy of "keeping our options open" is a bad one and that we should "consciously start closing" some of those options. This is true because "they draw energy and commitment" away from activities that promise greater success.

Erik Weihenmayer is the first and only blind man to reach the summit of Mount Everest. "When asked if anything was possible, Weihenmayer answered, 'No, there are limits. I mean, I can't drive a car. But there are good questions and bad questions in life. The bad questions are what if questions. What if I were smarter, or stronger? What if I could see? Those are dead-end questions. A good question is, 'how do I do as much as I can with what I have?'" Similarly, John Wooden said "do not let what you cannot do interfere with what you can do."

Our weaknesses and limitations are not a bad thing because they rule out options for us and make it easier to focus on the areas where we can be truly successful. Limitations are liberating. Because of this, we should appreciate them.

The Freak Factor

According to the Heath Brothers, authors of *Made to Stick*, openly admitting limitations even helps us build trust with others. This is true when discussing our own limitations or those of our ideas, products or services. "We've all come across salespeople who are reluctant to admit any weakness in their product or service, no matter how insignificant. As many a sales guru has pointed out, building trust involves being candid, and being candid involves admitting that your products aren't flawless. Admitting weakness can, oddly enough, make your core ideas more powerful."

Freak Profile: Allan Bacon

Allan Bacon is on a mission to help smart, creative people find their callings without having to quit their jobs. He the creator of GenerousNetworking. com and Avocationist.com and has been featured on CNN, the Dallas Morning News and the Christian Science Monitor. Below, Allan shares his weaknesses and how appreciating these apparent flaws helped him to build a fulfilling life, career and business.

"My first weakness is that I'm too social. When I was on a YMCA soccer team as a child I got the 'Ma Bell Gossip Award' because all I wanted to do was talk to everyone. My second weakness is that I cannot make myself do something that I think is boring. So instead of just raking the leaves, I spent an afternoon trying to figure out a way to rig up a giant tarp to load up all the leaves on. It didn't work and it took three times as long as just raking the leaves.

My third weakness is that as soon as I figure something out, I get bored. The tarp idea didn't lead to some break-through solution to the leaves. It just made it more painful to get the yard cleaned up. I still had to rake them. Now I just hire someone to do my yard. Ricky loves what he does and my yard looks way better than it ever did when I did it.

When it came time for me to have a career, my inability to do boring stuff and my tendency to get bored quickly became real issues. The problem was that I got bored every 1-2 years as I figured out each new job. And I lived in a place where there weren't a lot of jobs for a person with a PhD in Physics.

3. appreciation

So I got really good at changing careers. I turned my weakness of wanting to figure everything out into the skill of understanding how to change. I used the fact that I am 'too social' as a strength by meeting lots of new people. After several of these changes I realized that the traditional career approach wouldn't help me find something that really tapped into all of my passions.

Since I had trouble making myself do stuff I didn't understand, I had to come up with a new way to try out lots of things in a safe way. This led to developing the idea of Life Experiments where I figured out how to do anything I wanted to, like new careers, new hobbies and new jobs, without having to take a lot of time or spend a lot of money. One of these experiments was a blog I started as an excuse to meet more people and is my outlet for being 'too social'.

Instead of forcing myself to conform to a normal career path, I started trying lots of other ways to figure out what I love. Even though this was harder, it was the only way I could move forward, since I couldn't force myself to keep doing things I was bored with.

Now I get paid to figure things out, meet people and explain to them how things work. I write the Avocationist blog, speak, write and coach people on how to live their dream lives without having to put their incomes at risk. I also consult with entrepreneurs to figure out how they can get more business without having to invest a lot more money. Because it's my company I get to do lots of different things and add new things whenever I need to move on to something else."

Instead of trying to be perfect, we need to appreciate our limitations and make sure that we don't let what we cannot do interfere with what we can do. Then we need to go even farther. Once we've developed an appreciation for our weaknesses, we should amplify them.

4. amplification

exaggerate your weaknesses; don't eliminate them

If everything seems under control, you're not going fast enough.

– Mario Andretti

Many weaknesses are framed in terms of excess. We are told that we are too organized or too messy, too quiet or too loud, too critical or too kind. This chapter argues that this is usually incorrect. In fact, it is the opposite of the truth.

It is more likely that our problem is not because we have too much of any characteristic. Instead, we don't have enough of that characteristic. It is not because we emphasize it too much but because we emphasize it too little. The goal of this chapter isn't simply to help you accept your weaknesses; I want you to flaunt them, to parade them without shame.

We are so accustomed to disguise ourselves to others, that, in the end we become disguised to ourselves.

- Francois de La Rochefoucald

It can be difficult to amplify our weaknesses because we are often worried that we'll be rejected for being different. So we often try to moderate and control our weaknesses. Unfortunately, this inhibits our distinctiveness and hampers our success. It also prevents us from achieving our potential and becoming our truest self. The danger in trying to be what everyone else wants us to be is that we can forget who we are in the process.

Be Unreasonable

Seth Godin recently wrote about the danger of doing things within reason. "Within reason means, 'without bothering the boss, without taking a big risk, without taking the blame if we fail… be reasonable!' And so you do it half-heartedly and you fail. And who beats you? The people who did it without reason."

Most people would agree with the ideas in this book, as long as you don't take them too far. It is fine to build on your strengths, within reason. It is good to embrace your weaknesses, within reason. Go ahead and pursue your passion, within reason. Be yourself, within reason. But that is the problem. My point is that you need to go even farther in the direction that everyone is telling you not to go in.

Amplification is about being unreasonable, about doing things "without reason." If you can avoid the trap of doing things within reason, then you dramatically increase your chances for success. Next time someone encourages you to be reasonable, just realize that they are really asking you to be normal, average, mediocre and unremarkable. In other words, they are being unreasonable.

Michael Bungay Stanier, author of *Find Your Great Work*, has a cool video called 8 Irresistible Principles of Fun. Three of the principles reinforce the importance of amplification.

- Stop hiding who you are. *Figure out who you are, then turn up the volume.*
- Stop following the rules. *It's no longer about what you can't do, it's about what you can do.*
- Start scaring yourself. *Dip your toe into the bold, the outrageous and the unthinkable.*

There are three basic ways to amplify your weaknesses. You can brag about them, joke about them or exaggerate them.

Bragging

Sally Hogshead is a marketing consultant and author of *Fascinate: Your Seven Trigger to Persuasion and Captivation*. That's right. Her last name is Hogshead. Here is how she explains it on her business cards and website. "A hogshead is a barrel that holds 62 gallons. So what's your last name, smartass?" Sally didn't change her name and she doesn't attempt to gloss over it. She brags about it and when she's done you wish that you had a name as cool as hers.

> If you can't fix it, feature it.
>
> - **Gerald Weinberg,** *Secrets of Consulting*

Robert Merrill, author of the *Be Useful* blog, took me up on my challenge to define who he isn't and what he doesn't stand for.

He isn't competitive or assertive. He doesn't like telling people what to do, he doesn't make a great first impression and he doesn't handle stress well. He can brag about these weaknesses because they are clues to his strengths. For example, because he doesn't make a good first impression, he is "persistent in relationships and doesn't jump to conclusions."

The Freak Factor

He includes the following message for potential clients on his website. "If you invite me into the executive circle of your software-intensive business, you will probably find that I am different from most of you. That's precisely why I will be useful." Amplification goes beyond an internal appreciation of your weaknesses. It is about broadcasting them to others.

I am the proud father of three girls and no boys. When my youngest daughter, Sophia, was 11 months old, she wore an I'm Not a Boy shirt from Wry Baby. This is an important disclaimer because my children stay mostly bald until their third birthday and this leads people to identify them as boys.

The shirt was a gift from her aunt Amanda. Other shirts in the WryBaby collection proclaim proudly:

- I can't read
- I eat dirt
- I don't floss

This got me thinking. We need similar shirts for adults. We should be able to proudly proclaim what we are not. We should have t-shirts that brag about our weaknesses. Here are a few suggestions:

- I'm messy
- I'm not an athlete
- I can't do math
- I forget stuff
- I'm not creative
- I don't see the big picture
- I hate meetings

- I'm probably not listening to you right now
- I didn't shower today (or yesterday)
- I pick my nose (admit it, so do you)
- I don't have an iPhone
- I'm a nerd
- I talk with food in my mouth
- I eat dirt

What aren't you? What don't you do? Are you ready to brag about it? Are you ready to put it on your website or a t-shirt?

My friend, Stosh Walsh, is a trainer and coach for The Gallup Organization. Here are some of the quirks that he suggested for his t-shirt.

- I'm a perfectionist: I'm rarely satisfied.
- I'm too serious: I don't celebrate my accomplishments (or yours).
- I'm greedy: I think I can have my cake and eat it too.
- I'm selfish: My family is more important to me than my career.
- I'm an egghead: I want to know more, be more, and do more.
- I lack fashion sense: I wear nice suits, but I am not ashamed of my beard, even though it is not the same color as my hair

Freak Profile: Amber Osborne

The other day I got a comment on my blog from Amber Osborne, better known as Miss Destructo. Just read her bio below to see what it looks like when someone brags about their apparently negative qualities.

"Hailing from the swamps of Florida, currently starting a blue-haired revolution, in the mountains of Greenville, South Carolina. I am an ultra tall, sarcastically crass, swank, classy dame of the creative persuasion. My twenty plus odd years has formed me to be a world traveler, college graduate, award-winning writer, photographer, radio DJ and artist/event promoter. Also highly uncoordinated, somewhat of an insomniac, with a slight addiction to caffeine and music videos.

Six feet tall, blue hair, can type with my toes. My skin replicates faster than a normal person. Fully able to bend my thumbs and legs sideways and I have a rare bone in my sinus cavity. I am officially a mutant. When I was three I swore I had a computer in my head. I believed this till I saw an x-ray of my brain. That was only a few years ago.

Almost died at least twice. Once in a car accident, once by drowning. I don't drive and still hate the taste of saltwater. I can wake up without an alarm clock at an exact time. Most bathroom lighting hurts my eyes. I took chorus for most of my childhood. Piano for three years and I own a dulcimer. Out of all of this I can produce one hell of a rendition of Mary Had A Little Lamb."

In her recent blog post, Embrace the Pale, she encourages us to "love that part of you that is unique no matter how strange it is." If you've ever felt strange, Amber makes you wish that you were even stranger. Check her out at MissDestructo.com.

Joking

It's a good thing when people make fun of you. When I was a kid I got teased a lot. Other kids made fun of me because I was grotesquely skinny and looked like a candidate for a hunger relief poster. You could see my heart beating, even when I had a shirt on. My nicknames, in addition to those I've already shared, included doc, melvin, octopus, and many others. At the time, I didn't like having people make fun of me. I would guess that most people feel the same way, except for Scott.

Scott Ginsberg, author of *Hello, My Name is Scott*, is famous for wearing a name tag 24 hours a day, 7 days a week. He even had one tattooed on his chest, just in case the other ones peeled off. Scott believes that "parody often leads to profit." He argues that there are a lot of benefits to having people make fun of you or your business.

It is very difficult to get people to pay attention to you. Even though being teased might seem like a negative experience, it is still attention and attention is very valuable. As Scott explains, if people are making fun of you, it means that you are being:

- noticed
- remembered
- talked about
- imitated
- marketed

Is anyone making fun of you? Are you ready to encourage them, instead of trying to make them stop? How can you take advantage of the attention they are creating for you?

If no one else is doing it, are you willing to make fun of yourself? What is wrong with you? How can you show it off instead of trying to hide it?

Jimmy Vee is a consultant and the author of *Gravitational Marketing*. But he is known to most people as "the five-foot high marketing guy." He isn't ashamed of his height and he doesn't apologize for it. He doesn't see it as a weakness and he uses it to his advantage by calling attention to it. He paints a caricature of himself.

Another example is from Buckley's. Their cough syrup is nasty and they are proud of it. They aren't trying to hide it. Instead, they made the bad taste the focus of their advertising campaign by comparing it to trash bag leakage and sweaty gym socks. The tagline is "It tastes awful. And it works." However, the implicit message is that it works because it tastes awful.

Exaggerating

It takes courage to call attention to existing weaknesses but takes even more courage to make those weaknesses worse, to exaggerate them. That is what Hardee's did and it saved their company. I recently found this letter from Andy Puzder, President of Hardee's, on the back of the bag for my Philly Cheesesteak Thickburger.

"A few years ago when I became president of Hardee's Restaurants, we were selling so many things that we had truly become a 'jack of all trades and master of none.' Unfortunately, in today's competitive fast food world, that wasn't cutting it.

The chain needed to become known for doing something really well again… So I challenged my menu development folks to come up with a new line of burgers that would make people say 'Wow! I can't believe I can get burgers that good at a fast-food place.' And they did. They came up with 'Thickburgers.'"

It is important to note that Hardee's was going out of business and closing many of their stores before developing this new line of burgers. Even more importantly, most other fast food companies were furiously adding healthy options to their menu. In response to criticism about the negative health effects of their offerings, fast food outlets were offering water, fruit and salads. Hardee's moved in the opposite direction.

In essence, they were saying, "our food is fat and nasty and will make you fat and nasty." And it worked. They succeeded by amplifying the weaknesses of fast food while everyone else was busy trying to moderate those same weaknesses. They took fast food, which was already tremendously unhealthy and made it unhealthier. They took fatty foods and made them fattier. They took nasty food and made it nastier. And it worked.

Hardee's is not ashamed of the nutritional content of their food. They have embraced everything that is wrong with fast food because it is inseparable from everything that is right with fast food.

What would happen if you followed the example of Hardee's? What would happen if you started exaggerating the characteristics that others tell you to repair?

- Too loud? Do people tell you to quiet down? Don't. Get louder.
- Too organized? Get more organized.
- Too intense? Don't settle down. Get more intense.
- Not good at following orders? Find ways to be in charge.
- Too silly? Don't get more serious. Get sillier.
- Too childish? Don't get more mature, be more juvenile.
- Too nice? Don't get more assertive. Get nicer.

- Too messy? Don't start cleaning up. Get messier.
  - Too controlling? Find more stuff to control.
  - Too stubborn? Don't work on flexibility. Become even more committed.
  - Hyperactive? Don't become calmer. Become even more active.
  - Too lazy? Don't work harder. Find ways to do even less.

If people tell you that you do too much of anything, search for ways to do even more. If people tell you that you don't do enough of something, search for ways to do even less. Exaggerate your weaknesses.

You can only be young once. But you can always be immature.

– Dave Barry

Freak Profile: Joe Heuer

Joe Heuer is the Rock and Roll Guru. As he explains on his Twitter profile, @ RockandRollGuru, he is an author, speaker, humorist, rocker and nonconformist. If anyone has ever told you that you have to grow up in order to be successful, don't listen to them. Joe's story proves that you can grow older, wealthier and happier without growing up.

"My flaws are many, but I'll just share a few highlights. First, I'm psychologically unemployable. Among other things, that means I can't take orders. I come and go as I please and I only do stuff I consider fun. In other words, I do what I want when I want.

My mantra, as well as my business plan, is 'If you always do fun stuff, there will always be plenty of fun stuff to do.' This works incredibly well for me, as I'm allergic to doing stuff that's not fun. Consequently, I have the grooviest career, business and life I can imagine as the Rock and Roll Guru.

Another significant 'flaw' is my attention span, or lack thereof. The strength here is that I'm working on so much cool stuff that I never get bored. There's always another fun project to which I can turn my attention, however briefly. And since my maximum attention span is 90 minutes, I can harness my energy to deliver one of my two keynote addresses for that length of time."

We are all agreed that your theory is crazy.

The question which divides us is whether it is crazy enough to have a chance of being correct.

My own feeling is that it is not crazy enough.

- Neils Bohr to Wolfgang Pauli

Be Extreme

Are you a bad singer? Maybe you're not bad enough. Will Hung achieved fame as a contestant on American Idol, a reality show for aspiring singers. His singing was so bad that he caught the attention of the judges and the rest of America. He subsequently appeared on The Tonight Show with Jay Leno and the Today Show. Hung went on to record an album that sold almost 200,000 copies.

Are you too cynical? Maybe you are not cynical enough. The people at Despair.com have turned cynicism into a business by creating de-motivational posters, which parody the inspirational messages that decorate corporate conference rooms across the country. One of their posters caught my eye during the World Cup soccer frenzy. Below a photo of an injured soccer player it said, "Whining–If you expect to score points by whining, join a European soccer team."

Do you shop too much? Are you a shop-a-holic? Maybe you don't shop enough. Maybe you should find a way to shop more.

Maybe you should become a personal shopper. Work for people that are too busy to do their own shopping. Instead of spending your money, you could earn money, while spending someone else's money.

The Freak Factor

Do you eat too much? Maybe you don't eat enough. Do you eat too fast? Maybe you don't eat fast enough. Takeru Kobayashi has made a living out of speed-eating. He has set world records for eating hot dogs, hamburgers, bratwurst, lobster and dumplings. Kobayashi has turned gluttony into a career as a member of Major League Eating. I'm not making that up. There really is a professional association for speed eaters.

When the going gets weird, the weird turn pro.

– Hunter S. Thompson

Do you drink too much? Maybe you don't drink enough. Do you have a drinking problem? Maybe it's a drinking opportunity.

Zane Lamprey's new television show, *Three Sheets*, follows him "around the world, one drink at a time." He's getting paid to get drunk. Maybe you can turn your problem into a career, or fame, or both.

Are you too neurotic? Maybe you aren't neurotic enough. When Chris Martin of the band Coldplay was interviewed on 60 Minutes, the interviewer explained that Martin has a habit of making rules and writing notes and lists on everything, including his body and furniture. He concluded his description this way. "Like many artists he is openly, gloriously neurotic." Shortly after the interview, Coldplay won Grammy Awards for song of the year and rock album of the year.

It is tempting to believe that Chris and his band are successful despite his neuroticism. However, I think he is successful because he embraces and flaunts his neurotic impulses. I think we need to follow his example and be "openly and gloriously" weak. Just replace "neurotic" with your particular weakness and then ask yourself what you would do differently if you were going to do it openly and gloriously.

For example, I'm openly and gloriously hyperactive. After I ran my first 40-mile ultra-marathon, my brother-in-law told me that I was crazy and awesome. One of the main lessons of this book is that being crazy might be an important part of being awesome. But there is another important lesson in this example. Millions of children, mostly boys, spend their childhood being criticized for being hyperactive. I was no exception. I wished I could sit still, but I couldn't. I loved recess. I loved gym. I loved athletic practices and games. But my love of activity was considered a weakness.

Now, as an adult, I run marathons and ultra-marathons and compete in triathlons. When most people hear about my accomplishments, they say "Wow! I could never do that." Instead of seeing my hyperactivity as a problem, they see it as a strength they wished they had. This is an important turning point.

4. amplification

You will know that you have gone far enough, that you are amplifying your weaknesses, when people start to praise you for the very things that they used to criticize you for. You just have to go farther in the direction that everyone is telling you not to go.

Are you too fat? Maybe you aren't fat enough. Emme, Mo'Nique and Christina Lewis are openly and gloriously fat. Emme is a plus-size model that is proud of her appearance and has had considerable success because of it. Mo'Nique was the very large host of *F.A.T Chance*, a beauty contest and reality television show where full-figured women competed for the Fabulous And Thick (F.A.T) title. Christina Lewis runs the *Musings of a Fatshionista* blog and she describes herself as "fat and fancy as it gets." She never apologizes for her size and she shows other large women that they can be fat and still look fabulous.

I was looking for something to watch on TV last night and I couldn't help but notice a show on the Food Network called *Two Fat Ladies*. The show was exactly what you would expect. It was two fat ladies helping you make food that would make you fat.

One critic described the women as "overweight, badly dressed, and incapable of political correctness" making "dishes with bacon, lard, and fat." This description reminded me of Paula Deen, the famous and full-figured purveyor of southern-fried delicacies. When people criticize her because she uses such unhealthy ingredients, she has a standard response. "I'm your cook, not your doctor."

It also reminded me of a proverb that says, "Never trust a skinny chef." In other words, if the chef's food was really that good, they'd be eating more of it and it would show in their waistline.

It is important to remember that standards of beauty, as well as the value of many other characteristics, are artificially defined by society and have no basis in objective reality. A few hundred years ago, an attractive woman was fat and pale with black teeth. Being fat was considered beautiful because most people were thin and gaunt from a lack of food. Weight denoted wealth and health. Similarly, being pale meant that you didn't have to work outside in the harsh sun. Whiteness was so valuable that many people attempted to artificially whiten their skin, sometimes using lye and other toxic chemicals that eventually killed them. Black teeth were prized because they signified that you had access to sugar, an expensive luxury.

The new standard of beauty is skinny and tan with white teeth. Being thin denotes self-control, access to healthy food and the free time to devote to exercise. Bronze skin indicates that a person has free time to spend in the sun, instead of being trapped in a cubicle all day. It might also mean that they can afford artificial tanning services. White teeth show that a person is healthy and wealthy enough to afford good dental and orthodontic care.

The Freak Factor

Additionally, even though there is a general standard of beauty in society, there are certainly many people who are attracted to people who don't fit that mold. Just because everyone doesn't consider you to be beautiful, doesn't mean that no one does. This is just another example of why we can't allow other people to determine how we feel about ourselves. No one is perfect and sometimes we need to be the worst in some areas to be the best in others.

Be the Worst

Conventional wisdom says that we need to be balanced and well-rounded. We need to be strong in all areas in order to succeed. However, that isn't true. In fact, in order to be the best in one area you have to be willing to be the worst in others.

For example, while I was writing this book, Anthony Kim won the Shell Houston Open on the PGA Tour even though he had the worst driving accuracy of any golfer in the tournament. He wasn't just below average; he was the absolute worst.

Similarly, the two teams in the 2010 Super Bowl were the Indianapolis Colts and the New Orleans Saints. The Colts had the worst running game of any team in the NFL and the Saints had one of the worst defenses. However, the Colts also had one of the best passing offenses and the Saints made up for their poor defense with a league-leading offense. Both teams were the best in one area and the worst in another.

Shaquille O'Neal is more than seven-feet tall, weighs over 300 pounds and has missed more free throws than any other player in the history of the NBA. Because of this weakness, he has spent endless hours working with coaches to improve his skills. And he is still terrible.

He's so bad at free throws that other teams have developed a strategy for capitalizing on his weakness. They call it Hack-A-Shaq. They foul him before he has the opportunity to shoot so that he will have to score his points from the free throw line.

Since other teams implemented this strategy, O'Neal has led two different teams, the Los Angeles Lakers and the Miami Heat, to four NBA championships and has been an All-Star in each year of his career. In other words, Shaquille is one of the best basketball players of all-time, even though he is the worst free-throw shooter of all time. Actually, another player holds the record for the lowest free-throw percentage. His name is Wilt Chamberlain and he's considered by many to be the greatest player in NBA history.

Shaquille's gigantic hands make it very difficult for him to shoot effectively. However, his tremendous size also allows him to physically dominate and intimidate other players on offense and to block shots and get rebounds on defense. He is good at basketball because he is so big. He's also bad at free throws because he is so big. What makes him the best is also what makes him the worst. Similarly, if we want to be the best in one area, we need to allow ourselves to be the worst in other areas.

Brett Favre, former quarterback for the Green Bay Packers, won the NFL's Most Valuable Player award three years in a row. He also holds the record for the most consecutive starts as a quarterback. Additionally, he set the all-time NFL records for most touchdown passes, most completions and most passing yards in the same season that he set the record for the most interceptions. Like Shaquille's record for the most free throw attempts, Favre also has the most passing attempts of any quarterback.

Favre's gunslinger style, intensity and improvisation are what helped him set the touchdown record. Those same characteristics also led, inevitably to the interception record. Favre's strengths are his weaknesses. When you get one, you get the other.

Favre and O'Neal were the best in one area but the worst in another. Are you willing to allow yourself this same opportunity? You'll never become the best by fixing your weaknesses. Excellence requires you to amplify your strengths and allow your weaknesses to get even worse.

22-year-old Matthias Schlitte offers an even more interesting example of this principle. He began practicing arm-wrestling when he was 16 years old but has only been training the muscles in his right arm. When you see a picture of him, it looks like he has some sort of genetic deformity. His right forearm looks like Popeye's. It is nearly 18 inches around. But his left forearm looks like Olive Oyl's. It measures only measures 6 inches. It seems like the only muscles that he has are in his right arm.

This is a huge advantage in arm wrestling because his opponents are determined by weight class. His wrestling arm is much larger than that of his competitors because they have bodies with normal proportions. Unfortunately, this means that much of their weight is in parts of their bodies that don't help them with arm wrestling.

Schlitte can spend additional time and energy exercising his right arm because he doesn't have to bother with building the rest of his body. He is weak in many areas so that he can be incredibly strong in the area that is the most important. This makes him unbalanced but it also makes him successful.

Put all your eggs in one basket, and watch that basket!

- Mark Twain

Be Obsessed

Obsession is a word that has gotten a bad reputation. We use it most often in a negative way. The most notable example is the psychological diagnosis of Obsessive-Compulsive Disorder, which is so well known that most people just use the acronym OCD.

However, just as with the term freak, I think obsession can be a very positive thing. Successful people are obsessed with what they do.

In a recent Best Buy commercial an employee explains that he is a phone geek and he wants to help you understand what new communications technology can do for you. Who do you want helping you with your new phone, a geek that is obsessed with phones and technology and spends an inordinate amount of time learning about it, or someone who is just casually interested and has a variety of other pursuits? My guess is that you want the geek, the person who is obsessed with technology, not the well-rounded employee.

Mark Cuban, the billionaire owner of the Dallas Mavericks, recently posted 12 rules for start-up businesses on his blog. The first two rules are, "Don't start a company unless it's an obsession and something you love… If you have an exit strategy, it's not an obsession."

While I was running today, I got some inspiration from *I'm Not an Addict* by K's Choice. One of the most powerful lines comes near the end as the singer finally admits, "I'm not an addict, maybe that's a lie."

The lyrics reminded me of a story that I read in Runner's World magazine. The article explained how Rosie Coates, a six-foot tall, 300-pound, corrections worker, lost 110 pounds by running each day at 2:30am before leaving for work. She described her new passion for running this way, "it became an addictive thing for me. My ego totally rocks when I'm in motion--I feel healthy, empowered, happy, sexy and vibrant."

On the same page was a short feature, called Treadmill Junkie, that explained how Eminem has used running to help him get sober. "I was running twice a day for a while. It's like you go from one addiction to the next."

The next page included a short interview with Nate Jenkins, a runner who competed in the marathon World Championships on August 22, 2009. Jenkins runs three times a day and, at his peak, completed 190 miles in a single week. To put that distance in perspective, I also run marathons and I've run 250 miles… in the last seven months.

4. amplification

Coates, Eminem and Jenkins illustrate an important point. Addiction can be a very positive force. In fact, addiction might be an absolute necessity for world-class performance.

In his book, *Talent is Overrated*, Geoff Colvin explains that the superstars in every field, from sports to music to art, have one thing in common. It took at least ten years, or 10,000 hours, of intense and deliberate practice for them to become the best. In other words, they had to demonstrate and obsessive discipline in order to rise to the top. They had to become addicts.

I saw this obsession demonstrated vividly in the documentary, *Comedian*, featuring Jerry Seinfeld and Orny Adams. The film follows Seinfeld as he begins to re-build his stand-up comedy routine, with all-new material, after the phenomenal success of his TV show. Before touring with his new routine, Seinfeld spent more than six months perfecting each line late at night in basement comedy clubs throughout New York City.

And he wasn't alone. The most stunning part of the movie was seeing so many celebrities, who had more money than they'd ever be able to spend, still traveling the country trying to make people laugh. These are people that I thought had retired long ago to a beach in the Bahamas. Here are just a few:

- Bill Cosby, age 72
- Robert Klein, age 67
- Colin Quinn, MTV game-show host from 1987
- Ray Romano, star of *Everybody Loves Raymond*

They don't need the money, but they do need the laughs. They are addicts. To emphasize this point, the movie opens with this line from a comedy club owner. "There is a certain compulsion among stand-up comedians to go on-stage and perform." But don't mistake that compulsion for weakness. Their compulsion is an absolute necessity if they want to continue to be the funniest comedians in the world. Their compulsion, their addiction, is what drives them to obsessively and endlessly practice their craft. And it is that constant practice that makes them the best.

Freak Profile: Tom Morris

Tom Morris is a philosopher, public speaker and the author of numerous books on philosophy and business, including *The Art of Achievement* and *If Aristotle Ran General Motors*. We've corresponded about the freak factor concept for years and he's sent me quite a few of the quotes and examples in the book. One day he sent this personal example.

"On our exercise walk this morning, I told my son that I can see how a real weakness of mine, a tendency toward obsessive behavior (learning everything about and collecting fountain pens for a few years, then watches for a few years, then guitars for a few years and so on - and when the obsession is going full tilt, I'm thinking about it all the time, and then BOOM it's over and I'm on to the next phase - I also have a history especially in my grad school years, of finding a restaurant I love and going many times a week, and then never again or rarely ... when the phase ends) is responsible for my learning so much about something that I write a book on it or create a talk."

Freak Profile: Nance Rosen

Nance Rosen is a voracious and compulsive reader and seems quite proud of it. "I read a lot of things (publications, the backs of cereal boxes, anything except instructions to technology that I also am driven to purchase) that have no reason to be interesting to me other than the fact that my brain noisily demands to be fed, like the way your stomach spasms and makes noises when you're hungry.

I can't escape this drive to be relentlessly educated. It's why I can't wake up without lots of newspapers, real and online. It makes my Sunday ritual of having lunch out just an excuse to wend my way to a bookstore and come home with six books that I could probably get from a fellow publisher if I could wait (I run Pegasus Media World). My brain won't let me wait."

Her drive to read the backs of cereal boxes really resonates with me. Shortly after getting married, my wife cleared off the entire table during a meal and then asked, "do you have to read everything? What is so interesting about the back of the ketchup bottle?" It wasn't until later that I learned that one of my top five strength themes from the Strengthsfinder profile is Input. I just love to read. It is who I am.

Similarly, Rosen explains "If I'm not growing I feel like I'm dying. That's why being a lifelong learner isn't something that's nice for me, it's essential–like air, water and food." She needs to read. Like all of our strengths, this is both a blessing and a curse, a strength and a weakness. "My partners, clients, associates, fellow instructors, suppliers, employees, family and the panoply of people who surround me in my working life (which is 90% of my life) both benefit and suffer from my having this trait."

Nance ends the article with this question. "What is your driving trait? I've revealed mine in its most manic light, because I want you to see that the basis of your brand isn't a choice, it's your calling." In other words, your uniqueness and your greatest opportunity for success can be found in the activities that you are compelled to do, those that you simply can't avoid.

Nance's obsession with reading and learning serves her well in her career as an author, speaker and publisher. She has found and created an environment that rewards her for being herself. She can amplify and flaunt her apparent weakness because she has found the right spot. We'll talk about this more in the chapter on alignment.

Here is a short equation that summarizes all of these stories.

Addiction = Obsessive Practice = Greatness

Greatness starts with addiction. Without the addiction, without the obsession, without the compulsion, without the inescapable need, there is no practice and thus there is no greatness.

What are you addicted to? What do you need? What can't you live without? What do you do too much, too often and for too long?

How can you build on your addiction and become the best? How can you use the power of your addiction to fuel the obsessive practice that it takes to become one of the best in the world?

The Freak Factor

Outrageous Rewards

Sometimes we seem to confuse being "not bad" with being "good," but they're not the same thing. There are huge rewards for being good, especially for being the best. There is virtually no payoff for being mediocre or average.

What is it worth to be the best? Why bother trying to become the best? What's so bad about being average?

To answer those questions, let's consider book sales. If you write an average book, it will sell 500 copies. That is probably not even enough to cover the publishing and marketing costs. The vast majority of books, 90%, don't even do that well, selling less than 100 copies. As this example illustrates, it doesn't pay to be mediocre.

But what about bestsellers? What if you wrote a great book? The best books can sell more than a million copies. Authors of these books make enough from these sales to retire early and live on their own private island in the Caribbean. It is like winning the lottery. Do you want to be average or do you want to be the best?

The value of being the best can be seen more clearly by looking specifically at book sales of the leading online bookseller. Below are the average daily book sales based on sales rank:

Sales Rank	# Sold	Revenue
#1	2100	$4,200
#10	220	$440
#100	50	$100
#1,000	11	$22
#10,000	2	$4
#100,000	1	$2

The #1 book sold by the leading online bookseller moves more books in one day than the #100,000 book will sell in six years and more books in two days than the #10,000 book sells in an entire year! Even estimating a small royalty of $2 per book, the #1 book earns $4,200 per day for the author, while the #100,000 book earns just $730 per year for its author. There are exceptional rewards for being exceptional. These rewards increase drastically as you move closer to the top.

The same is true in the speaking business. Statistics from the National Speakers Association show that the top 5% of speakers earn more than $10,000 per presentation and the top 40% earn more than $5,000 per speech. These speakers earn more for one day's work than the average American earns in two months. Meanwhile, average speakers are paid in pens, plaques, gift certificates, mugs, and honorariums that barely cover their travel costs.

Entertainers and professional athletes provide even more astonishing examples. An all-conference high school baseball player will probably get a scholarship to college, avoiding school loans and other costs that most students face. If that same player can become an all-conference or all-American in college, they will probably be drafted by a professional team.

Once drafted, they will start in the minor leagues, where salaries are low and crowds are sparse. Notice that the rewards for being very good are sometimes very small. But if a player does well in the minor leagues, they might get a chance to play in the big show, Major League Baseball. The minimum salary for a major league player was $380,000 in 2007. That is more than ten times what the average American earns in a year. The average salary for players was almost $3,000,000, more than 100 times the salary of the average American.

But the rewards are even more outrageous if you are the best of the best.

Alex Rodriguez was the highest paid baseball player in 2007, earning just under $28,000,000. It would take the average American more than 1000 years to earn this amount. Even when compared to other professional baseball players, his salary is still enormous. A player, who earned the league minimum, would need to play for 72 years in order to catch up with Rodriguez's yearly paycheck. The average player would need nine years to match the same total, which is problematic since the average career lasts less than three years.

It is far more lucrative to leverage your strengths, instead of attempting to fix all the chinks in your armor.

– Tim Ferriss, *The Four-Hour Work Week*

The following chart illustrates three important points. First, rewards increase exponentially as you go from being very good to being the best. Second, there are virtually no rewards for moving from below average to average. Third, your best chance at being the best is to build on your existing strengths, where you are already above average, instead of trying to remediate weaknesses, where you are below average.

The Freak Factor

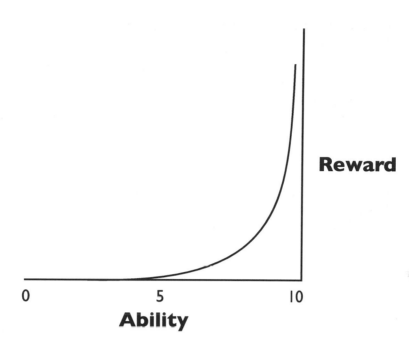

The rewards for being first are enormous. It's not a linear scale.
It's not a matter of getting a little more after giving a little more.
It's a curve, and a steep one.

- Seth Godin, *The Dip*

Be Strong

There are three myths that keep us from building on our existing strengths. First, we believe strengths will always be there so we don't need to worry about them. But the truth is that if you don't use it, you lose it. Second, we think that since we're already strong in these areas, there's not much room to improve. But the truth is that our strengths are where we have the most potential.

More than thirty years ago, the Board of Education in Omaha, Nebraska tested the reading comprehension of high school freshmen. They discovered that some students could only read 90 words per minute with good comprehension, while others could read 350 words per minute with the same level of comprehension. They put all the students in an Evelyn Wood Speed Reading course to improve their skills. At the end of six weeks, the students who were weak readers and could only read 90 words per minute had improved to 150 words per minute.

However, the students who were already strong readers improved their scores dramatically from 350 words per minute to almost 3000 words per minute. We often think that we should work on our weaknesses because we have more room to improve in those areas. But this study shows that our greatest opportunity for improvement lies in our existing strengths.

Third, some people are worried that focusing on strengths will make them one-dimensional. Mark Twain once said that "To a man with a hammer, everything looks like a nail." His point was that we sometimes use the skills that we have in situations in which they aren't relevant or appropriate. Twain has a lot of great quotes but I'd like to modify this one slightly.

"If you are a person with a hammer, start looking for nails." This is the essence of amplification. Use what you have. Don't worry about the strengths that you don't have. Seek out more situations that require what you possess. Find more things that need hammering. Find people with a broken hammer or no hammer. They need someone just like you. As Seth Godin suggests, if "a hammer is exactly the tool that will solve your problem… Hire a guy who only uses a hammer. Odds are, he's pretty good at it… Go to someone who has only one tool, but uses it beautifully."

There is another reason that we don't need to be worried about becoming one-dimensional. We have more than one strength. The ultimate success strategy is combine your strengths together into a superpower to become a superfreak. For example, my top five strengths, as identified by Gallup's StrengthsFinder profile, are:

- Input–I love to learn and read
- Ideation–I love ideas
- Command–I love to be in charge
- Activator–I love to get things moving
- Achiever–I love to get things done

I combine all these strengths into a superpower in my work as a professional speaker. Speaking gives me the opportunity to share the ideas (Ideation) that I've learned by reading and listening to audiobooks (Input). Being the one at the front of the room with a microphone in my hand makes me the center of attention. Everyone is listening to me (Command). The fact that I'm self-employed also fulfills my need to be in charge. Additionally, I don't need external motivation to keep my speaking business going because I'm so motivated to work on projects (Activator) and complete those projects (Achiever). I'm a superfreak.

Furthermore, we need to remember that our strengths are patterns of passion and proficiency. They are what we love to do. They are what we do well. They are also broad abilities, not narrow skills. I can apply my Command strength in all sorts of ways and in many different situations. There are a lot of ways to take control.

I can focus my Input strength on a variety of topics. My Ideation strength allows me to see the connections between seemingly different concepts. Building our strengths doesn't make us one-dimensional because our strengths have many dimensions.

Freak Profile: Clemens Rettich

If you're still worried that sticking with your strengths will make you one-dimensional, just read about Clemens. His experience shows that we can be strong, while still moving in many directions. In fact, your strength might be that you love to move in so many different directions.

"It started in grade 2. My teacher Mrs. Hannah once turned to me in exasperation, saying 'You don't have to be such a know-it-all.' I had probably answered a question of hers with something half-baked that I had gleaned from a book somewhere.

It was 1967. My family had just moved down from northern British Columbia the year prior, not long after we had emigrated from Germany for a second time. At the age of 8, I read voraciously. Books, comics, cereal boxes. Anything. Text was a drug.

Somewhere in there, I began my journey of almost getting everywhere. Therein lays the weakness I have struggled with for years: I find everything interesting; every avenue has intersections and branches to follow. I get bored and struggle to see anything through to the end. I know just enough about almost anything to be dangerous.

I pick up so many things and then put them down. Family and friends always wondered if I would ever focus. Degrees, businesses, places I lived, events and activities, always completely committed (for a day, or a month, or a year). I learned like a sponge but always got bored and moved on before ever getting to Malcolm Gladwell's 10,000-hour mark of real expertise.

Languages came easily if I tried: music, French, Latin, poetry, computer languages and management. But I never mastered any of them. By the time I hit my 40's I was starting to wonder. So were a lot of people around me. I wasn't alone in feeling that my inability to focus and to commit for the long haul was serious weaknesses.

I trained in improvisational theatre for 2 years with the Vancouver Theatre Sports League. I did two years of performing arts at Simon Fraser University, working collaboratively with artists, dancers and musicians. More languages. I worked for five years in a letterpress shop as a typesetter and printer. That's a language where you learn to read and design upside down and backwards. Then I moved away from the big city.

On the Queen Charlotte Islands (Haida Gwaii) for 15 years, I taught and did community development work, directed a music festival, produced a CD, raised two kids and managed staff. I traveled every year for more training and to lead workshops in improvisation, team building, and leadership around British Columbia. I focused on the language of Positive Behaviour Support. As a high school principal I worked with the Haida First Nation to develop a multi-agency intervention team for aboriginal youth. Then I got a business degree, an MBA in executive management from Royal Roads. I spent three years marketing educational programs in Japan, China, Hong Kong, Taiwan, South Korea, Germany, Spain, and Brazil.

But early on, even in the constant shifting, I was already conscious of something. I was comfortable everywhere and could make almost anyone else comfortable too: physics majors who played cello, loggers who played hard, teenagers who trusted no one, chefs, mathematicians, politicians, athletes, gay punkers, and bankers. It didn't matter whom I sat down with, I knew just enough about their world that I could find a place to connect and start a conversation. And I knew how to listen.

Now I have a career as a coach that has, at its heart, the ability to connect dots and think outside the box. I am old enough to have learned to bring complete focus to someone for two hours without blinking. Listening has become a contact sport for me and I play hard.

I think the key to making a difference is learning how to listen. Most of my clients' major breakthroughs were not the result of anything I said, in any language; they were the result of what they said in a place where they actually got to hear themselves think… and I just listened.

My strength also lies in my layers of experience and education. I make connections others don't make. I see patterns and trends and possibilities. I don't believe in rigid plans but believe passionately in having a focused, crystal clear vision of the future. After years as a business owner, manager, and team leader, I know that leadership and management are a craft and an art more than a science. And I understand what that actually means. Where other people talk about creativity, and thinking outside the box, I have lived outside the box my whole life.

Now everything I went through makes sense: the endless indiscriminate reading, the meandering journey through music, the sciences, performance, business, education, sports, management, art, writing, and the fascination with what everyone else does. Just like then, I ask questions to allow others to connect the dots that I see hanging in the air. I create safe spaces to have conversations outside the box, because I have always been comfortable there.

Sometimes I look back and regret how long it took me to get here. Wouldn't it be cool to have an extra decade to really enjoy this? But, as a number of friends and supporters have said, I wouldn't have been ready. I couldn't be who I am without my past. I couldn't do what I do now as well as I do, if my so-called weaknesses had not shaped me and my journey."

There are three primary reasons to build a career around your existing strengths. First, it feels good. It is enjoyable and energizing to work on our strengths. Second, as we just learned, the rewards for improving our strengths are outrageous.

> Your strengths have the capacity to become so dominant that they render your limitations irrelevant.
>
> — Dr. Lance Watson

Third, our strengths make up for our weaknesses. A well-developed strength often makes our weaknesses irrelevant. As Keith Ferrazzi explains in *Never Eat Alone*, "In developing an expertise that highlighted my strengths, I was able to overcome my weaknesses. The trick is not to work obsessively on the skills and talents you lack but to focus and cultivate your strengths so that your weaknesses matter less."

> Success is achieved by developing our strengths, not eliminating our weaknesses.
>
> - Marilyn vos Savant

Nick Morgan is the author of *Trust Me: Four Steps to Authenticity and Charisma*. He also writes an excellent blog with tips for effective speaking at PublicWords.com. One of his recent posts is about dealing with a negative audience. Our natural inclination might be to start with the dissenters in the audience and try to win them over but that is the opposite of what he suggests.

His first suggestion is to "talk to the positive people in the room… This is counter-intuitive, but important, because if you can establish a positive relationship with a few people in the room, that positive feeling will ripple across the crowd. We have these things called mirror neurons in our brains that give us essentially the same experience as we see the people around us having. So if we see someone reacting positively, we will too."

This same advice also applies to our own lives. Too often we focus on the negative aspects of our life and/or work and try to tackle the problems and weaknesses first. Instead, we should focus first on the positive elements of our lives and then the success and confidence we gain in those areas will ripple across the other parts of our lives as well. If you use this strategy, you'll be surprised to find that, after starting with the positives, the negatives seem to disappear or at least become less problematic by the time you eventually get to them.

> When everyone is against you, it means that you are absolutely wrong—or absolutely right.
>
> - Albert Guinon

Be a Reject

Alex Bogusky and his ad agency, Crispin Porter + Bogusky, are the creators of some of the most well-known and successful advertising campaigns of the last few years. His successes include the resurrection of Burger King and the introduction of the Mini car to America. A recent profile in Fast Company explained that "his control-freak tendencies are widely known - and desired - by clients."

He doesn't just amplify his own weaknesses; He does the same for his clients. "Instead of hiding qualities that may seem negative - such as Mini's tiny proportions or Burger King's fat content - Crispin exploits them. 'It's part of your job as a marketer to find the truths in a company, and you let them shine through in whatever weird way it might be.' Naturally, that risks pissing someone off."

Amplifying your weaknesses leads to resistance. As Bogusky warns, "life conspires to beat the rebel out of you."

The Freak Factor

If you spend your days avoiding failure by doing not much worth criticizing, you'll never have a shot at success.

- Seth Godin

If we believe that we can please everyone by becoming perfect, by fixing all of our weaknesses, we will fail. If we imagine that it is possible that everyone will like us, respect us and appreciate us, we will fail. The best are rejects. Not everyone likes Starbucks or McDonald's or Apple or Wal-Mart. It's true that a lot of people do, but not everyone does. We can't make everyone happy and it is futile to try.

I cannot give you the formula for success, but I can give you the formula for failure, which is to try to please everybody.

— Herbert B. Swope

As Seth Godin explains, "If you are willing to satisfy people with good enough, you can make just about everybody happy. If you delight people and create change that lasts, you're going to offend those that hate change in all its forms. Your choice."

Notice that he said "you can make just about everybody happy." Good enough doesn't make everyone happy and often it doesn't make the right people happy.

Ignore everybody.

- Hugh MacLeod, *Gaping Void*

Success is about making the right people happy. It is about delighting the right people and being willing to make other people unhappy. You have to decide who the right people are, but the right people and most people are not always synonymous.

Someone will always be unhappy with what you do. The great thing is that you can often decide who will be happy and who will be unhappy.

What will you choose? Are you willing to offend some people? Or will you settle for good enough?

Judy Rey Wasserman, an artist at UngravenImage.com, wrote the following comment in response to my blog post about rejection. "Artists deal with rejection often, whatever their field. Real artists have something unique to offer, and that means different and untested, so gatekeepers are wary. As a fine artist (with a manifesto to a whole new way of creating art focusing on the stroke), I researched other artists, now revered, to help me withstand rejection. I discovered that van Gogh (never recognized in his own lifetime), Rembrandt, the original Impressionists, and the initial Cubists, Warhol and many, many others all experienced great rejection by the establishment. Rejection can be a good sign that one is doing something innovative! So now I sail forth less concerned about rejection."

> The notion, that everyone can be everything to everybody at all times, is completely off the mark.
>
> — Keith Ferrazzi

Celebrity chef, Rachel Ray, doesn't mind being criticized. "If you spend so much time thinking about the people who dislike what it is you're doing, you're doing a disservice to the people that employ you. I'm not employed by those people. I work for the people that want the type of food I write [about], the type of food we share with people."

It's easy to give this advice but a little harder to take when it happens to you. Last year I got my first piece of hate mail, or at least nasty mail. Most people like my seminars and classes, and most of my work is based on referrals from happy participants and meeting planners. I've always known that everyone doesn't appreciate my style and I've seen some scattered negative evaluations over the years. But it was a challenge to respond positively, both internally and externally, when someone attacked me directly in an email.

I have to admit that it bothered me a lot in the beginning. I wanted to challenge their arguments. I wanted to address each issue and show them that they were wrong. But that would have been a waste of time. Just as we don't need to fix our weaknesses, we don't need to try to please all of our critics. Just as we should build on our strengths, we are probably better off building deeper relationships with our existing fans than trying to convert our enemies.

So I didn't reply. I didn't respond. I took my own advice and reframed the attack as evidence that I'm on the right track. I still don't like it and I'm not looking forward to the next piece of hate mail. But maybe I should. Maybe I should measure my success by how many people I please and how many people I offend. Maybe if everyone seems happy, then I'm doing something wrong.

How about you? Are you getting enough hate mail?

In case you wonder what a personal attack looks like, I've included the email below.

"Dave: I attended one of your seminars and I felt uncomfortable with how much of your talk was regurgitation of other people's ideas. You arrogantly stated, "and now I get paid to talk." Well, never forget that it is a privilege to talk to people. No one stays awake at night in anticipation of hearing you and no one stays awake at night after hearing you either I promise. Just to give you a reality check because I think you need one.

You claim that you have associates ????? Mmmmmhmmmm. You claim that you have refreshing solutions ?????? Revive dead ideas of others is more accurate. Authentic and humble??? Apparently this is only for others to practice.

I just think it is important to get a sense of perspective that your message and style does not really sit well with everyone and I think it is great that you have selected the 'best comments' to put on your website to impress others with; but I hope you do some deep introspection about your true level of rigor and originality. Good luck mr leadership. LP"

Do not fear to be eccentric in opinion, for every opinion now accepted was once eccentric.

– Bertrand Russell

In response to an audition on American Idol, Simon Cowell offered this feedback to Amy. "There are a lot of people who will like you and a lot of people who will find you very annoying." I think that is true for most of us and it's something to get comfortable with.

You can please all of the people some of the time and some of the people all of the time, but you can't please all of the people all of the time.

- John Lydgate

When I ask audiences to list the greatest leaders of all time, a few names always make the list: Abraham Lincoln, Martin Luther King, Jr., Jesus Christ, Gandhi, John F. Kennedy. These leaders were indeed great and they've had a lasting influence. However, they are all similar in one other way. They were all killed. They were loved and admired by millions but also hated and despised by millions more. Their lives and violent deaths are a testament to the fact that we can't please everyone. In fact, it seems that the more some people love us, the more others will hate us. I've illustrated this in the diagram below.

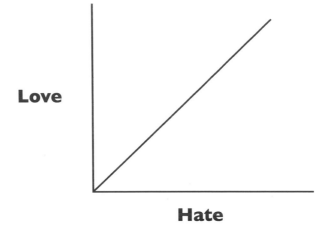

Seth Godin refers to leaders who challenge the status quo as "heretics." I saw Seth give a live presentation on his book, *Tribes*, in 2009. He was definitely a freak, showing off his mismatched socks and sporting lime-green Buddy Holly glasses. If you didn't know him and you saw him on the street, you might laugh and dismiss him as a dork. But that would be a mistake.

He is one of the best speakers that I've seen. In particular, his slides were unique, funny, emotional and imaginative. He argued that "heretics are the new leaders. The ones who challenge the status quo, who get out in front of their tribes, who create movements. The marketplace now rewards (and embraces) the heretics. It's clearly more fun to create the rules than to follow them, and for the first time, it's also profitable, powerful and productive to do just that… Suddenly, heretics, troublemakers, and change agents aren't merely thorns in our side - they are the keys to our success." He also offered some great advice for aspiring freaks.

- Don't just copy what works for Seth. You are different. His tactics might not work for you.
- Be a positive deviant. Find where you are both different and successful, then build on that.
- Everyone won't join your tribe. Get over it. Find your audience and turn them into fans.
- Do something that people can criticize. Be a heretic. Challenge the orthodoxy.
- You can have a small, tightly knit tribe or a large tribe. But you can't have both.

I want to follow up on his last point. Even if we can't please everyone, we can still choose a small group of people and find ways to please them. Kevin Kelly, at The Technium blog, argues that all you need to be successful is 1,000 True Fans. That isn't even close to everyone. In fact, it's almost no one. It is less than .01% of the population of the United States. Some people have that many friends on Facebook. We'll talk more about this in the chapter on affiliation.

Controversy is good. Don't be afraid to polarize people.

- Guy Kawasaki

I'll take it one step further. If we just need to please a few people, then this means we can succeed even if the vast majority of people don't like us. We can be successful even if almost everyone dislikes us. The Heath Brothers make this point very clearly in a Fast Company article called *Polarize Me*. They suggest that "if you want people to like you, first decide who needs to hate you." Don't just choose who to please, choose who you will displease. Intentionally select a group or groups that you do not intend to help or satisfy. How many of us are ready to implement that suggestion?

Jason Seiden, at JasonSeiden.com, encourages his readers to "fail spectacularly." I love his post entitled, *Embrace Excellence, Not Arrogance. What Stupid Advice*, in which he described an executive who is facing resistance within a new organization. "When you've got someone who is good at his job, who knows it, who is willing to use power to move things along, who is not tolerant of convention born from thoughtless routine, and who pushes others to break the mold, that person will be interpreted as both arrogant and excellent." In other words, polarization is almost unavoidable.

As I've explained before, I got in trouble a lot in school for talking too much, being hyperactive, making jokes and failing to do what I was told to do. In 8th grade, I was in a very small art class. There were only four or five students. Most of our class time was spent drawing or painting, while the teacher sat at her desk. There wasn't a lot of lecture in art class.

I took it upon myself to fill the silence. I offered a running commentary about my art-work, told funny stories and made jokes. Unfortunately, the teacher did not think I was funny. She did not like me at all. I may, in fact, have been the most irritating person she had ever met. At one point, she petitioned the principal to have me spanked. My parents had to approve the request and they were glad to do so. But the beating didn't work and our problems continued. One day she sent me out of class and told me to stand in the hallway for the rest of the period. As I walked out she said, "I think we are all tired of listening to you."

The rest of the students in the class quickly talked amongst themselves and decided that they weren't tired of listening to me. I was very entertaining. They loved it. The prospect of an entire class period without me was not appealing. They told the teacher that they liked my ramblings and asked her to reconsider her decision to expel me from the classroom. As you can probably guess, this caused the teacher to like me even less that she already did.

There's an important lesson here. The same thing that causes some people to like you, will cause other people to dislike you. The same thing that makes some people happy, will make other people unhappy.

Getting a lot of people to hate you is easy. All you have to do is become really successful doing what you love.

- Hugh MacCleod, *Gaping Void*

Unfortunately, as Pam Slim explains, it is our personal success and happiness might actually cause others to dislike us. "As much as we talk about wanting to be happy and fulfilled, when you actually are, it can annoy the crap out of those around you." This is because our happiness will often remind other people how unhappy they are.

The best are not universally popular. They are rejects. The formula for failure is to try to please everyone. Here is the formula for success. First, don't try to please everyone. Second, choose a few people and focus on pleasing them. Third, choose a lot of people and focus on offending them.

Whatever the public criticizes in you, cultivate. It is you.

— Jean Cocteau

Freak Profile: Roxy Allen

Roxy Allen is a great example of someone who has learned to amplify her apparent weaknesses. Her story shows the power in cultivating what others criticize.

"It is simple: I like to talk. I was voted 'Most Talkative' in high school. I would get in trouble a lot in high school for talking during class or staging a protest against something I didn't believe in or planning a way to get out of class by pretending I had a chess tournament to go to.

My mom teased me through college for holding too many 'forums.' She and my brother are introverts. On the Myers-Briggs Type Inventory she and my brother are both ISTJ and I am ENFP, the exact opposite.

I also like to stand out. I wear my hair in a natural curly tapered 'fro and sometimes it gets really frizzy. People like to touch it and tell me it feels like a sheep or a dog. That used to make me uncomfortable but now I embrace it because it makes me stand out.

I try to embrace my talkative side by finding outlets for it. I like to talk to interesting people. When I visit the Newseum in DC, I attend their lecture series that features famous authors and politicians. This summer I met Juan Williams of NPR and Cokie Roberts. I like to ask them questions and get real answers. After asking Juan a question about the future of journalism, many people came up to me, even at the Starbucks across the street, and told me what a good and important question I asked.

But it is not all serious for me. I met Ace Young from American Idol's Season 5 on tour because I liked him so much. It's fun to meet people with good stories. A good question also got me into *O Magazine*. They published my letter to the editor in their April 2008 edition where I wrote in about an article by Suzy Welch and she responded to it. I am now blogging about the people I have met and hope to meet and I have a goal to interview and/or personally meet the author of every book and blog I read."

Roxy was criticized for being outgoing, talkative and inquisitive. However, instead of trying to minimize those characteristics, she is actively seeking ways to amplify them. Her goal is to become more outgoing, more talkative and more inquisitive. She's going farther in the direction that everyone told her not to go, and finding success in the

4. amplification

process. Her most recent project is a newsletter for people seeking jobs in international Non-Governmental Organizations (NGOs). You can find her at RoxyAllen.com.

Reflect

- What is one of your supposed weaknesses?
- Choose one that you routinely apologize for.
- Instead of apologizing for it, how could you flaunt it?
- How could you demonstrate that you are comfortable with this aspect of your life and that you don't plan to change?
- Reflect on a time when you were able to put your strengths to work.
- How did it feel?
- What were the results?

The Freak Factor

5. alignment

don't try to fit in; find the right fit

Every individual has a place to fill in the world and is important
in some respect, whether he chooses to be so or not.

- Nathaniel Hawthorne

If we are going to amplify our weaknesses, then we also need to move into situations that maximize our strengths and make our weaknesses either irrelevant or powerful.

The Elephant Man

Joseph (John) Merrick live in England during the late 1800's and was widely known as the Elephant Man. Due to his severe deformities, he was considered unemployable and spent much of his life as an attraction in a freak show. After the English government banned freak shows, he was befriended by Frederick Treves, a physician at London Hospital. Merrick was treated with kindness by the hospital staff and many visitors and he lived there until his death.

However, because of his grotesque appearance, he did not anticipate that anyone would ever accept him. When he first arrived at the hospital, he asked Treves to help him find shelter at an asylum for the blind. He believed, quite correctly, that his major weakness, physical abnormality, would not be a problem if he could live among people who couldn't see. He knew that how he looked would be irrelevant to the blind residents of the asylum. Furthermore, with the visual barrier removed, those residents would be able to truly "see" him and accept him for his many positive qualities.

This is an extreme illustration of alignment. Instead of fixing our weaknesses, we can find situations that make them invisible.

Think about Merrick's former life. As a freak show attraction, there was, quite literally, a spotlight on his weakness. In a home for the blind, that spotlight would be extinguished, only to be replaced by a new light that could be focused on his strengths.

Hide not your strengths. They were for use made.
What's a sundial in the shade?

- Benjamin Franklin

A Sundial in the Shade

A sundial tells the time by casting a shadow, across its face, which points to a particular hour. Direct sunlight is an absolute necessity for a sundial to function. If it is in the shade, it won't work. But it would be a mistake to think it was broken and an even bigger mistake to try to fix it. In fact, any attempt to fix the sundial will probably damage it. The sundial is simply in the wrong spot and needs to be moved into the sun.

Many of us are sundials in the shade. Things aren't working, but we are not broken. We are just in the wrong spot. We need to move out of the shade and into the sun, or we need to start chopping down trees.

Theodore Roosevelt, the 26th President of the United States, once encouraged his audience to "Do what you can, with what you have, where you are." I agree with the first two parts of that statement, but not the last. If you are doing what you can, with what you have and it isn't working, then maybe it's time to leave where you are and go somewhere else.

A similar maxim is "Bloom where you're planted." This is bad advice because we aren't plants. We aren't rooted to a single spot. We have the ability to move and we should take advantage of that.

And even if we were plants, it is still bad advice. If a plant is in the wrong spot, it won't bloom at all. Trees, flowers and other vegetation illustrate the important of our environment. If it's too hot, too cold, too bright or too dark, the plant can't survive. There's nothing wrong with the plant. The problem is the plant's location. Plants thrive when their environment matches their unique needs and characteristics. The same is true for us.

That is why I came up with a new saying that emphasizes the importance of alignment. "Plant yourself where you can bloom."

Michael Jordan was one of the greatest basketball players of all-time but then he retired and began a new career in baseball. He failed in this new pursuit and couldn't even make it out of the minor leagues. Following this failure, he returned to basketball and won three more NBA championships. His experience shows that greatness in one area doesn't necessarily generalize to other situations. A great champion in one sport was a complete failure in another. Baseball was his shade and basketball was his sunlight.

Sally Hogshead is the author of *Radical Careering: 100 Truths to Jumpstart Your Job, Your Career and Your Life*. Three of her radical truths argue that we should stop trying to fit in and start freaking out.

Radical Truth #19: Being in a crap job isn't your fault. Staying in a crap job is. No matter how bad things seem, you're never without options. If your current job doesn't fit, remember that you have a choice. You can find something better.

Radical Truth #85: Jump and a net will appear. It's impossible to be successful when you cling to obsolete situations out of fear. Only when you put yourself out there wholeheartedly can the best opportunities present themselves.

Radical Truth #99: Expressing your truest self is the ultimate competitive advantage. Traditional corporate culture requires fitting in. But fitting in is standard, and boring. Who you are is the most powerful differentiator you could ever possible hope for.

What happens when we force ourselves to fit in? Paul Graham has a great illustration of the negative effects of being in the wrong environment. "I was in Africa last year and saw a lot of animals in the wild that I'd only seen in zoos before. It was remarkable how different they seemed. Particularly lions. Lions in the wild seem about ten times more alive. They're like different animals. I suspect that working for oneself feels better to humans in much the same way that living in the wild must feel better to a wide-ranging predator like a lion. Life in a zoo is easier, but it isn't the life they were designed for."

Have you ever been frustrated with your work and said, "this place is a zoo." Maybe it is a zoo and maybe you are unhappy in your job because you weren't designed to be caged. Maybe there is nothing wrong with you. You are just in the wrong environment.

Pam Slim believes that "each of us has natural, organic preferences for how we feel most alive, relaxed, happy, and passionate at work." We feel alive when we find an environment that fits these preferences. Our desires are natural and organic; we don't need to change them. We need to acknowledge them and adapt our lives to them. A lion doesn't need to learn how to live in the zoo. He needs to find the open plains and live the life he was made for.

When we resist the urge to accept our natural preferences and fail to find the right fit, it can be tremendously painful. Pam Slim says it's like "wearing a shoe two sizes too small. Your ideal situation is like wearing a pair of size eight wide shoes of a stylish, comfortable brand that feels custom-made for your foot and looks sexy too. Your current situation is like wearing a pair of size six narrow shoes, in an unflattering material, with a heel that is both ungainly and unattractive. So why in the world do we try to jam our foot into an unattractive, uncomfortable shoe, otherwise known as our day job?"

A man who trims himself to suit everybody
will soon whittle himself away.

— **Charles M. Schwab,** *Bethlehem Steel*

Consider this brutal example from Cinderella, not the Disney version. "Cinderella's stepmother instructs her daughters: 'Listen,' said the mother secretly. 'Take this knife, and if the slipper is too tight, just cut off part of your foot. It will hurt a little, but what harm is that? The pain will soon pass, and then one of you will be queen.'"

If your shoes didn't fit, would you find new ones or would you repeatedly jam your foot inside them, hoping to someday adapt? Would you blame yourself or blame your shoes? Would you change yourself or change your shoes? Should you quit your job? Maybe. If it doesn't fit. The alternative is even more painful.

Instead of fixing our weaknesses, we need to look for the right fit. We need to find situations that match our strengths, highlight our abilities, and bring out the best in us.

The first essential in a boy's career is to find out what he's fitted
for, what he's most capable of doing and doing with a relish.

— **Charles M. Schwab,** *Bethlehem Steel*

The Rudolph Principle

Last year, I was watching the classic TV version of *Rudolph the Red-Nosed Reindeer* and realized that it beautifully illustrates the importance of alignment, finding the right fit.

Just let the song run through your head for a minute.

"Rudolph the red-nosed reindeer had a very shiny nose, and if you ever saw it, you would even say it glows."

Rudolph was different. He had a major and obvious flaw. He was a freak. This is the same for most of us. We are different. We have flaws. We are too impatient or too messy or too organized or too serious or too loud or too quiet. We are freaks.

"All of the other reindeer used to laugh and call him names. They never let poor Rudolph, join in any reindeer games."

The Freak Factor

Rudolph's flaw made him unpopular and led to his rejection and isolation. No one wants to be rejected. So what do we do? We often try to hide our flaws and fix our weaknesses. We become ashamed. We wish we could just be normal, like everyone else. We want to be accepted, so we try to change.

This is just what Rudolph and his parents tried to do. They covered up his nose with a black rubber cone, but it didn't work. The red nose still shone through. It looked like Rudolph was destined for a life of pain and misery, but then the situation changed.

"Then one foggy Christmas Eve, Santa came to say, Rudolph with your nose so bright, won't you guide my sleigh tonight?"

Rudolph's nose wasn't really a weakness. It was a strength in disguise. In the right situation, a "foggy Christmas Eve," Rudolph's nose was an irreplaceable advantage. When the situation changed, the value of his unique characteristic changed as well.

What made him a freak also made him a hero. He didn't succeed in spite of his weakness; he succeeded because of his weakness. What would have happened if Rudolph would have gone to Hollywood and gotten a nose job?

"Then all the reindeer loved him and they shouted out with glee, Rudolph the Red-Nosed Reindeer, you'll go down in history."

Rudolph's legacy, his enduring fame, was a result of a perfect fit between his unique qualities and the situation. Do you want to succeed? Do you want to make history or at least make a difference? Find your foggy Christmas Eve. Look to your apparent weaknesses and flaws. They are strengths in disguise. They offer clues to how you can make a unique contribution. Don't try to hide them or fix them. Just find the right situation, the one that offers the perfect fit between who you are and what is required. Unlike Rudolph, we don't have to just wait for the right situation to come along, we can seek it out or even create it.

Arianne Cohen is 6'3" and the author of *The Tall Book*, which explores her experiences as an unusually tall person. She understands what it's like to be different and have everyone staring at you. She also understands the importance of finding the right situation for your unique characteristics. "Though I was hyper self-conscious at school, I was never remotely self-conscious on a pool deck, because there my long arms and legs had something to do–I had some sort of use for all that tallness. It was a valued tool."

I think normality is whatever the majority decides it will be, and in our company people with autism are the norm.

— **Thorkil Sonne,** *CEO of Specialisterne*

Thorkil Sonne is the founder of Specialisterne, a Danish software-testing company. He started the company because his son has autism and Sonne wanted him to have a meaningful job. Nearly 75% of the company's employees have some form of autism, but Sonne doesn't hire them because he's trying to be charitable. He hires them because their disability is the perfect fit for the work his company does.

Sonne explains that his "ambition was to use the autism characteristics as a competitive advantage." His company's work matches the unique skill sets of people with autism spectrum disorders with a major need in the field of software and game testing. Symptoms of autism include intense focus, high tolerance for repetition, and a strong memory. These are the same skills that are necessary to be effective as a software tester. When people with autism work at Specialisterne, they're not disabled; they're uniquely qualified.

It is hard to love being different until you discover the one place in the world where you are not different.

Arianne Cohen, *The Tall Book*

Yahoo! employs a similarly unconventional approach to find people who are uniquely qualified to give the company feedback on their new services. They're not looking for nice, kind or pleasant individuals. Their invitation asks, "Fussy? Opinionated? Impossible to please? Perfect. Join Yahoo!'s user panel and lay it on us."

My object in living is to unite my avocation and my vocation.

- **Robert Frost,** *Two Tramps in Mud Time*

I've run a few ultra-marathons in the last five years. During my training, my brother-in-law sent me an ESPN.com article that asked, "Are these runners ultra-tough or ultra-crazy." One of the quotes that stuck out to me was from Yiannis Kouros, a Greek ultra-marathon runner and the current record-holder for every distance from 100 to 1000 miles. He doesn't think ultra running is for everyone.

The Freak Factor

"Ultra running is a metaphysical event. If you don't have that kind of idiosyncrasy, you will never become an ultra runner, even if you train all your life. I am one of those people who recommend and try to inspire people to get involved with running. But ultra is not a fun-running sport–it's only for unique souls."

I think this is true for more than just ultra-marathon runners. Certain activities seem perfectly designed for certain people. A fulfilling life involves discovering meaningful pursuits that match the idiosyncrasy of our souls.

Four Elements of Fit

Jonathan Fields, author of *Career Renegade*, challenges traditional definitions of career success and offers a new standard. "Will this career allow me to: Spend the greatest amount of time, absorbed in activities and relationships that fill me up, while surrounding myself with people I cannot get enough of, and earning enough to live comfortably in the world?"

There are four elements of finding the right fit. The first is *passion*. What do you love? What energizes and inspires you? The second is *proficiency*. What are your skills? Where do you excel? The third is *payment*. How can you get compensated for activities that combine both your passion and proficiency? How can you make a living doing what you love? The final component is *purpose*. How can you make a difference? How can you make a positive contribution? It is possible to design a meaningful and fulfilling career that includes all of these elements.

The sequence of these four elements is important. Most people address them in the wrong order. They start with payment. How can I make the most money? Then they move on to proficiency. Can I do it? This is followed by passion. Can I tolerate the job requirements? Finally, some consider the question of purpose. Will this activity cause anyone harm? Unfortunately, this approach usually leads to frustration and failure. Passion comes first.

Passion

Sometimes pursuing our passion will allow us discover unexpected ways to get paid to do what we love. Matt Harding loved to travel so he saved up, quit his job and took a trip around the world. He recorded his trip by filming himself dancing at many of the famous locations he visited like Machu Picchu, Easter Island and the Great Barrier Reef (underwater). The YouTube video of his dances went viral eventually capturing more than 33,000,000 views.

Because of his tremendous popularity, Stride gum, sponsored his video allowing him to travel the world again. This time he traveled to 42 countries over the course of 14 months and created another dancing video, which you can find at WheretheHellisMatt.com.

He also starred in Visa's *Travel Happy* campaign and has appeared on *Good Morning America* as well as numerous other media outlets.

What have you always wanted to do? Why haven't you done it yet? There are no guarantees that pursuing your passion will lead to a new business or career but Matt's story shows that it is possible and that sometimes the journey becomes the destination.

Famous Freak: Will Shortz

I was flipping through the channels the other night and got distracted by my laptop. That happens a lot. When I looked up, I realized that I'd inadvertently stopped on C-SPAN, which was televising a graduation ceremony at Indiana University. The commencement speaker was Will Shortz, editor of the crossword puzzle for the New York Times.

I thought he was joking when he said that he had a degree in enigmatology. He wasn't. Apparently, he is the only person on earth who holds this degree in the study of puzzles. He went on to say, "What I've always enjoyed most was making and solving puzzles… In eighth grade, when I was asked what I wanted to do with my life, I wrote 'professional puzzle maker.' The problem was a career in puzzles didn't seem possible because puzzles typically don't pay much."

When he asked a well-known puzzle designer about pursuing a puzzling career he was told, "'Don't do it. There's no money in it. You'll starve.' . . Fortunately, I didn't give up my dream… My advice for you is, first, figure out what you enjoy doing most in life and then try to do it full-time. Life is short. Follow your passion. Don't get stuck doing something you don't enjoy."

Will's experience shows that payment follows passion, not the other way around.

Unfortunately, we've been taught that work isn't supposed to be fun; that is why they call it work. However, it is possible to experience enjoyment, meaning and fulfillment at work.

If you're still not sure which career is right for you, check out Sean Aiken at OneWeekJob.com for some ideas. He did a different job each week for a year. One week he was a host at an aquarium. The next week he was a fashion buyer. Each week he posted a video of his experience and wrote about it on his blog.

Purpose

Tad Agoglia owned a very successful crane company that made him a millionaire. But he wanted more than money. He wanted meaning. So he started *First Response Team of America*, a nonprofit emergency management team. They track weather patterns and move quickly to the scene of floods, tornadoes and hurricanes. Tad uses his past experience by bringing heavy equipment, satellite communications and generators to communities that have been devastated. In 2008, he was chosen as one of CNN's Heroes. It might seem unusual for someone to find purpose as a crane operator, but as he explains, "we all have something to give."

Scott Harrison was an event planner. He made a lot of money and had a lot of fun organizing parties for rich and famous people and for the companies that sponsored him. Unfortunately, his success wasn't making him happy. He wanted to do something that mattered. After a trip to Africa, he started *Charity:Water*, a nonprofit organization that provides wells to communities throughout the world. Now he uses his connections with influential people and his marketing skills to promote a cause that saves people's lives. He has combined passion, purpose, proficiency and payment.

Three Pepperdine University graduates, Mike Marriner, Brian McAllister and Nathan Gebard, were unsure what to do for a living. So they started accepting every credit card offer that they got in the mail, packed up an old RV and traveled across the country on a road trip. What made their trip unique was that they stopped along the way to interview people who were both successful and passionate about their work. Their first interviews included Michael Dell, Sandra Day O'Connor, and Manny the Lobsterman.

They filmed each of these extraordinary encounters and this led to the birth of *Road Trip Nation*. Interviews from the first trip became a documentary on PBS as well as a book, *Finding the Open Road,* and a DVD. The three founders then created an organization that allows other students to travel the country and interview inspiring people. They started by searching for their own road and now they are helping other people who are searching for their own road in life. A new nonprofit arm of their organization is also helping high school students discover their unique path. Mike, Brian and Nathan found their purpose in helping other people to find their purpose.

Freak Profile: Joel Rodell

Joel and I became friends in college, where he was famous for his talent show performances, which included the electric pickle and wrapping most of his body in duct tape. Here is how he describes himself.

"I am a mess. I am disorderly. I lose things. I talk over people and don't listen very well. I have grand ideas, but have a hard time following through with them. If I spent time actually caring about this list, I would have no time to do what I do best, which is building relationships with my family, friends, customers and employees. My focus has now moved towards those things I excel at, not the things that have hampered me for years."

Joel designs and installs playgrounds for PG Playgrounds in Kansas. He feels that this is what he was put on the earth to do and that he is serving others. The tagline for his company is "making playgrounds matter." He recently completed a project in Greensburg, Kansas, where the entire town was destroyed by a tornado. He also installed a boundless playground that is accessible for children with disabilities and helped a family build a playground in memory of their young daughter who recently passed away. Joel is making the world a better place, one playground at a time. His work is meaningful. It has purpose.

Seven Ways to Find the Right Work

The most common question that I get after my seminar is, "do I have to quit my job to find my freak factor?" In other words, people want to flaunt their weaknesses, but they are afraid of how it will affect their existing career and personal finances. Craig Houston at CareerGuyd.com has a good perspective on this question. Instead of answering it directly, he challenges people to examine the real consequences of staying in the wrong job. "Are you stuck in a job and afraid to leave because of the security it provides for your family? If the job makes you miserable, what are you really providing for your family anyway?" As Pam Slim explains, "If you continually repress your natural desires, you will find yourself in a permanent 'living dead' state, so used to choking down your emotions that you can no longer access them."

Craig argues that "your energy and presence is perhaps the most significant gift you can provide (to your family). The truth is, when you have found the most fitting work, it makes you feel incredible. Would you like to feel like a rock star or superhero every day? Imagine what that would do for every aspect of your life."Chris Ferdinandi at Renegade HR argues that many potential rock stars appear to be below average or mediocre because they're "in the wrong position that isn't well aligned with their passions and strengths." Similarly, Laurie Ruettimann at Punk Rock HR says that if you've just had a less than positive assessment from your boss, don't freak out. Instead, "think about a new job. Think about a new career. Think about living the kind of life where it doesn't matter what your boss or supervisor thinks about you."

Below are seven options for finding or creating a better fit between your unique characteristics and your work. They are listed in order of difficulty and the degree to which they will disrupt your life. The easiest options are first and the harder ones follow.

Alignment isn't an all or nothing proposition. Take a look at the strategies below and start with the one that you are most comfortable with. The point is to start somewhere and start now.

1. Keep your job and pursue your passion through hobbies, volunteering or family involvement.

 If you can find positive outlets for your unique qualities, your work will seem more bearable. This is the route that Allan Bacon suggests. His blog, Avocationist.com, offers tips for pursuing your passion without quitting your job.

If you're not passionate about your job, find work away
from your paid job that makes you come alive.

- Sital Ruparelia

I met Allan at Pam Slim's *Escape from Cubicle Nation* event last summer in Charlotte. His article, *Moving to Paris without Quitting My Day Job*, offers some great ideas for finding your passion by performing Life Experiments.

"When I wake up I can look through the opening in the heavy drapes and see that I am still here. Cool, it wasn't a dream.

I see the 1800s Haussmann-style townhouse across the street from our Paris apartment and I hear the sounds of Vespa scooters blaring down the street and shopkeepers talking as they open for business. Then I remember that I have three weeks to go living in the leafy 16th arrondissement with my wife and three daughters–for free, without taking vacation and without quitting my job.

I couldn't have even conceived of this just three years earlier. Back then I was miserable in a corporate job. A snapshot: one night I couldn't sleep because I was so stressed about work. So what did I do? I got up and went to work–at 4 am. When I walked into the office I expected quiet. So I was surprised when I heard the clicking of keyboards and saw the lights on in several cubicles. At this company, everyone knew the trick of sending late night emails to 'prove' our value as hardworking and committed to the company. I just didn't realize so many of those emails were coming from the office.

So, how did a 40-year-old average guy find his way from wee-hours corporate email suck-up to paid Parisian expat in three years? I needed to learn three seemingly oxymoronic approaches to break the unspoken "rules" of the conformist career path.

A. To keep moving forward, go backward

Why did I stay in my crazy corporate environment? Because it was so good! Seriously. I had great pay, a big bonus, growth potential and benefits. I'd have to be crazy to leave that, right? Unfortunately, it was the environment that was making me crazy–it was like I was diving without a snorkel–the harder I tried to move forward, the more stressed I got and the less I could breathe.

So what did I do? I gave up. I did the unthinkable and went backwards on the career ladder. I went back to a job at a company I had had five years previously. Now instead of just a snorkel, I felt like I had a giant air tank on my back. Everything was easier and I had much more room to think and explore other options for my career.

Surprisingly, even though I had the same job, I learned that I was not the same person. I knew more and could add more value. Within a year my salary was higher than it had been at my old job, I was making a much bigger impact and I was starting to see new possibilities for myself. I was diving deeper and seeing more fish.

B. To understand your passions, don't analyze, experiment

Have you ever changed careers? The best approaches I could find used tests and coaching and analysis to help you look back at your history and then find the next step to a job that would make you happier. These never seemed to help me make the type of big change I was looking for.

It was the equivalent of trying to decide whether I would like mango ice cream by analyzing my past food choices. If I were doing it career-planning style, it would go something like this:

OK, let's look at what you've liked in the past–vanilla, strawberry–great. And let's have you fill out what tastes you like. We'll analyze these and rate you on the "Sweet/Tangy" scale. Then we'll have you read a summary of the mango flavor. OK, based on those you need to decide whether to switch over to mango from vanilla.

I needed a way to actually take a taste of the areas that might bring me more satisfaction. How could I actually try being a DJ or a professional photographer without putting my whole family at risk? And how could I do it in very little time and with almost no cost?

I needed a way to take a bite-sized taste of different parts of life. I needed to be able to do Life Experiments.

C. To find more satisfying work, focus on playing

About this same time, another realization hit me. Work is a terrible place to find your calling. Just like the career tests limited me to my past work experience, my job limited me to my current role in the company. I guess I could have offered to DJ the company holiday party, but I didn't see them letting me spend four hours a week doing that.

Back when I was a kid, we didn't need to do any analysis to try something new. We just did it. When I wanted to be a radio DJ in 5th grade, I took my turntable to my friend Brian's house. With our two turntables and a microphone we mixed a complete radio show: music, jokes, call-ins and shout-outs. When we played the tape at school, my teacher snorted because she was laughing so hard.

Notice what we didn't do: we didn't just dream about being DJs and we didn't read about DJs and we didn't interview a DJ. We were DJs. As kids, there were no limits to what jobs we could 'try on.'

So I started doing Life Experiments by working them into the cracks and crevices of my busy schedule outside of work: visiting art galleries on a lunch break, taking photos on the weekend, exploring Tokyo paper shops between sales calls on a business trip. My guiding principle was to find the fastest, cheapest way to take action and try the essence of all the interests and job ideas I had.

All of these experiments gave me more and more ideas and more and more confidence in what was right for me. Eventually I realized that my wife and I could probably find a way to experiment with living abroad. *Et voilà, Paris.*

D. Finding Your Own "Paris"

The impact of these Life Experiments was way out of proportion to the effort. On a flight back from Asia, it hit me that the part of my job that mattered most to my company was when I was face-to-face with customers. And that it didn't really matter where my office was. So instead of taking my kids on a crazy, bleary-eyed tour across Europe, I decided that we should find a way to actually live there long enough to get a taste for what the experience would be like. Would we kill each other in a city apartment? Would we get bored? Would we go crazy from having to learn how to navigate in a place where we didn't speak the language?

Of course, none of those things happened. Our Paris trip was done by a house swap with a French family. I used Home Exchange and highly recommend it. In Paris, my daughters learned that not everyone around the world saw things the way we do, and they began imagining a whole new set of possibilities for their future. I arranged my business meetings for Europe while I was there–my company saved money and my customers were happy to have quick access to me.

The benefits impacted all aspects of my life. As I continued my Life Experiments, things started happening faster than I could have ever imagined. Each thing led to several new things. I had started my Avocationist blog about a year before I left work. The original purpose was to share helpful stories with others going through transitions. But as I interviewed people for the blog and I continued my own explorations, I realized that I needed to share the lessons I had learned with a bigger audience.

I applied one of my own big messages and made the mental shift to seeing work as a means to an end instead of the main focus on my life. I had some money saved up and then I negotiated an agreement with my employer to consult with them a day a week. This kept money coming in and gave me more time to work on speaking, writing and doing seminars. It's only one year past Paris and I'm writing a book and consulting, no longer working in a company at all.

It's never too late to become a Nonconformist. Don't quit your job. Just quit thinking. Start experimenting. It will change your life."

2. Keep your job and adapt your responsibilities to focus more on activities that you enjoy and do well and less on those you dislike and do poorly.

This step requires a good relationship with your supervisor. If you have this conversation, you need to focus on the benefit that the department and company will experience if you are allowed to adjust your role. Marcus Buckingham has a lot of wonderful examples of how this has been done effectively in his book, *Go Put Your Strengths to Work*.

Success is not defined by position or pay scale but by this:
doing the most what you do best.

— Max Lucado

Elad Sherf posted this comment my blog. "It is important to ask yourself how many hours per day you do things that you like and that you are good at? Most people don't enjoy 100% of their work. The question is, 'what is the figure for you?'"

He's right. Most people don't enjoy everything about their jobs. Instead of trying to find the perfect job or business, we should strive to increase the number of hours per day that we can apply our strengths and decrease the number of hours each day that we spend in our areas of weakness. Here are seven suggestions to get you started.

A. Review your workday and approximate the percentage of time that you spend in your areas of strength and weakness

Is it 20% strength and 80% weakness? Is it 50% strength and 50% weakness? A student once told me that her job required her to spend just 10% of her time in areas of strength and 90% in areas of weakness.

B. List the specific activities that allow you to do what you do best and those that put a spotlight on your flaws

- What tasks do you love to do?
- When do you lose track of time?
- What type of work are you consistently recognized and praised for?
- What tasks do you hate to do?
- When does time seem to stand still?
- What type of work do you consistently struggle with?

C. Schedule more activities that draw on your strengths.

- Do you have the authority to make these decisions?
- Do you need to involve your supervisor?
- Do you need the cooperation of your co-workers?

D. Eliminate tasks that draw on your flaws.

- Is the task essential?
- Can you get help from someone?
- Can you exchange tasks with a co-worker that has complementary strengths?

We'll talk more about these strategies in the chapters on affiliation and avoidance.

E. Set a target

If your current state is 20% strength and 80% weakness, then maybe 50/50 is a worthwhile goal. Even a small change in this percentage will pay large dividends in energy, motivation and results. This, in turn, will help you to make it through the parts of your job that are less desirable.

F. Refuse the next promotion

Laurence Peter is the creator of *The Peter Principle*, which states "every employee tends to rise to their level of incompetence." In other words, we move up in organizations until we find ourselves unable to do the work that is required.

I think this is true and that there is a simple explanation. People who are successful get promoted. Unfortunately, the positions that they are promoted into often require different strengths than those they possess. As they move up, they gradually move farther away from the situations that made them successful, the situations that fit their unique characteristics.

The best example is the salesperson who becomes the sales manager. The strengths, and corresponding weaknesses, of a great salesperson aren't necessarily suited to effective management. Because of this reality, we need to be more concerned about finding the right fit than about moving up. Moving up often means moving out of our sweet spot and might actually undermine our long-term success.

G. Ask for a demotion

This might seem like a crazy suggestion, but if being promoted is sometimes undesirable, maybe we should be looking for a demotion. Allan Bacon calls this "strategic downshifting," which he explains below.

"Here's my radical suggestion for creating more time and flexibility in your job: give yourself a demotion from management to a position where you can directly make a strategic contribution. Just like downshifting in a car, this gives you more power and control. It also makes your engine rev higher and gives you faster acceleration. That is to say, you can create a place where you can be excited about your work again. I've done this three times in my career and I know of dozens of others who have had similar experiences. There are several factors to a successful downshift.

First, find a place where you are excited and can see new possibilities. After we sold a company where I was VP of Sales & Marketing, I was excited about applying our new parent company's licensing business model to our old industry. I knew it was a chance to influence a significant change in the way optics were sold for cell phone cameras. But I couldn't do it from my management role. Instead, I took responsibility for leading the business development efforts by myself with no team.

Second, look at previous jobs to find great launching pads. Bob got passed over for a promotion early in his career at GE. Instead of continuing to press for a management role, he focused his productivity on inventing new products. He had a happy and sane 40-year career there and was awarded over 50 patents. The guy who beat him out for the management job was let go 6 months later in a restructuring effort.

Third, build a new constituency to support your efforts. Work with your management to ensure a graceful transition. Even more importantly, make sure that you have support from people excited about what you will be doing in your new (old) role. They can help smooth over any resistance you encounter.

Fourth, watch out for the pull back into management. Traditional advice says that taking a step backwards on the career ladder means that you are done for. This is exactly the opposite of my experience. I have found that the wisdom and passion you bring to a downshifted role tends to bring results and recognition. My shift to a direct sales role netted me a bonus within 6 months."

Allan isn't the only one who found the right fit by getting demoted. A local television station in Baltimore hired a young African-American woman to co-anchor the evening news. Unfortunately, they believed that she was too emotional and not detached enough to be a big city news anchor. When she flubbed a line, she'd laugh. When a story was sad, she'd cry.

There were several things about her appearance the station didn't like. So they decided to demote her to an early morning talk show. And that morning show was the perfect fit for Oprah Winfrey's personality. Getting demoted was the best thing that ever happened to her.

3. Keep your job and start a part-time business during your evenings and weekends.

You can make a lot of progress on an entrepreneurial venture without ever quitting your job. It can also be helpful and wise to explore the viability of your business concept before giving up your full-time income. Your day job will be much more bearable if you have the hope of someday leaving to pursue your business full-time. Pam Slim's book, *Escape from Cubicle Nation*, is a helpful guide.

Pam cautions that, even though leaving your job is risky, staying in your job isn't safe either. The current economic downturn and rising unemployment rate are painful reminders of this fact. Because of this, you need to be ready to leave your employer, especially because your employer might leave you first.

"As I watched formerly high-flying corporate employees slink out of their offices with their personal effects in cardboard boxes, I asked myself: 'Who feels better today, those employees who put all of their effort into their job, or those who took the time to develop a wide social network, invest in self-development, and pursue a small business on the side?'

Probably the easiest way to turn your passion into your job is to do it gradually. If possible, don't quit your day job before launching your business. If you want to podcast, start with a monthly show or with a very short weekly show and see how it works. If you want to open up a yogurt shop, take a part-time job in someone else's yogurt shop and learn everything you can about how to run the business.

If you're passionate enough, it won't even feel like work. In many cases, if your idea is a good one, you'll eventually become so busy or successful in your part-time endeavor that it will be clear when you should quit your day job and become a full-time independent business owner."

Yesterday I got a call from Bob Fink at *Educational Resources of MN*. During our conversation, he explained that he has developed a tremendously successful business while continuing his job as a fourth grade teacher. He started small and built his business steadily during the evenings and weekends.

Pam Slim has ten other great suggestions for getting started, without leaving your job.

1. Take responsibility for your decision to keep your job.

2. Learn as much as you can during the workday.

3. Look for projects that relate to your business idea.

4. Find a mentor and/or coach.

5. Network with other entrepreneurs and potential customers.

6. Attend conferences and workshops.

7. Take advantage of your company's tuition reimbursement policy.

8. Get out of debt.

9. Save up six-months of living expenses.

10. Simplify your life and reduce your monthly expenses.

The last three tips related to personal finances are especially important. You're not really afraid of losing your job. You're afraid of being unable to pay your bills. By increasing your savings account and reducing debts and living expenses, you are reducing the probability that your business will fail. This is because your new business won't have to generate nearly as much profit as it would if you didn't follow these three steps. Don't make it harder than it has to be. Adjust your lifestyle, at least in the beginning, to fit your dreams of becoming an entrepreneur.

4. Stay at your company but request a transfer to a new job that matches your skills and interests.

For example, maybe you're working in accounting but feel that your creativity is being stifled by all the rules and regulations and your innovative ideas are seen as dangerous and unwise. A transfer to the marketing department or to a new program development position might change people's perceptions of the value that you bring to the company and give you a greater sense of fulfillment.

Kate took this approach and it worked for her. Here is the story that she sent to me.

"I have been contemplating applying for a different position at work. After I read your *Freak Factor* manifesto, a coworker stopped me in the hallway and encouraged me to consider it. And I thought that it would be wise that I consider taking a job that emphasized my strengths and worked with my weaknesses. So I updated my resume this weekend and I'm submitting it today."

She applied for the job, completed two interviews and was hired. Now she has a position that is a better fit for her. She has a job that lets her do what she does best every day. She didn't try to force herself to get better at a job she didn't like. Instead, she looked for, and found, a better fit for her unique characteristics at the same company.

5. If you can't find the right fit at your current employer, then quit and find a new full-time job.

Identify the kinds of activities that put the spotlight on your strengths and make your weaknesses invisible or irrelevant. Look for jobs that include those activities and start applying. Obviously, this isn't easy but the results will make the process worthwhile. Dan Schawbel's personal branding book, *Me 2.0*, has some very useful advice and resources on how you can move your career in a new direction.

I also found a great illustration of this strategy in an advertisement for Fleet Feet Sports, a running apparel retail chain.

"MARTA IS SLOW. She used to be a barista. A really slow barista. She wanted the coffee to be really good, her boss wanted it to be really fast. He fired her. We hired her. Now she takes her time finding the right shoes for our customers. They don't mind the wait. You can't hurry fit."

Marta had an apparent weakness. She was slow. But her slowness wasn't a weakness. It was just a bad fit for her situation. It wasn't the right fit for a job as a barista.

She didn't need to get faster. She didn't need to hurry up. She needed to get out. She needed to find a job that valued her unique style, one that valued patience and attention to detail.

She found that job at Fleet Feet Sports. They don't want her to change. They don't want her to fix her weakness. In fact, they don't see it as a weakness at all. They see it as an essential qualification for the job.

If you are struggling in your current job, if you are on the verge of being fired, you might need to change your job instead of trying to change yourself. If you are fast, impatient, hurried, anxious or frenzied, find a job that values speed. If you are slow, lazy, unmotivated, particular, perfectionistic, detail-oriented or analytical, find a job that values accuracy, quality and patience.

You'll be happier. Your former employer will be happier. Your new employer will be happier. What could be better?

6. Quit your full-time job, get a part-time job and start a new business.

Some people aren't cut out to be employees. If your freak factor requires you to do your own thing but you are somewhat risk-averse, this strategy can give you a greater sense of security and a modest source of income while you get your business off the ground. You can also get a new full-time job that is more flexible or has less responsibility and will allow you more time and/or energy to focus on your new business. My job as a college professor gives me a tremendous amount of freedom to pursue my business as a speaker, trainer and author.

As a manager I always struggled with the details. I had no shortage of ideas and goals for the future but didn't always follow them up with specific implementation plans. Because of this, my bosses regularly encouraged me to spend more time focused on operations and less time developing new programs. Despite their prodding, I could never seem to motivate myself to dig in to the day-to-day management of the department. This seems like a clear weakness and to some extent it was in that particular situation.

However, my inability to manage the details is offset by my abilities as a strategic thinker. For example, I designed a new program to provide employment services to 200 people with disabilities and initiated a $2 million capital campaign and building project in my first year on the job. My abilities were highly valued by my bosses, but they still wanted me to balance my big picture focus with an appreciation for operational issues. They appreciated my strength but didn't see its connection to my weakness. At some point, I realized that the job just wasn't a good fit for my particular style.

I left management to become a professor and a consultant. Now I teach business strategy and help my clients with strategic planning. No one criticizes me any more for failing to handle the details, because they hired me to help them see the big picture. My new environment highlights the positive aspects of my characteristics and minimizes the negative aspects of those same characteristics. In order to be more successful, you don't have to change yourself, you just need to change the situation.

7. Quit your job and start a business.

If your weaknesses include impulsiveness, over-confidence or idealism, then this is the option for you. If you have no fear and you just want to make the leap right now, then go for it. I strongly believe that the best way to find the right fit is to create it. No employer will ever care as much about your future than you will and they won't ever be able to creatively adapt to your unique characteristics as well as you can.

Jonathan Fields' book, *Career Renegade*, has some very practical and exciting examples of how people have turned their passion into a viable business. For example, one husband and father turned his love of video games into a thriving business writing books of tips and tricks for conquering new games.

Fields rejects the belief that jobs are the safe choice and entrepreneurship is risky. "As long as you're working for someone else, you'll never have the control you want." Additionally, your employer has priorities that can often conflict with your needs. "What's best for you is not their driving motivation."

It's essentially impossible to become successful or well-off doing a job that is described and measured by someone else…

The only way… to get ahead is this: Make new rules. People who make up new rules continue to be in short supply.

- Seth Godin

From the beginning of time, most people were self-employed. They lived as farmers and hunters and had great freedom in deciding how and when to do their work. Organizations, managers and employees, in contrast, are a relatively new phenomenon. When factory jobs were first introduced in England, most people referred to them as "wage slavery." I believe that people aren't designed to be employees and that working for others usually diminishes your happiness, fulfillment and financial success.

Additionally, current trends in society and technology are making it more feasible to become a successful entrepreneur. Jonathan Fields challenges us to consider "What might unfold if you identified what you loved to do first, then tapped the wealth of tools, strategies and technologies that have only come onto the scene in the last few years to build a substantial living around what makes your entire life smile?"

Scott Adams was unhappy with his corporate job. So, he quit. His *Dilbert* cartoon, which offers a scathing critique of most companies and their managers, has become one of the most popular in the country. He would never have had this same level of success as a cubicle dweller.

If you're considering entrepreneurship, the following questions might be helpful.

- What specialized knowledge and skills do you already possess?
- How could those skills be translated into a business?
- Why does your current company employ you?
- What valuable service do you provide?
- How could you provide that same service to your company and/or other companies as a free agent?
- Are there examples of other people who have already done this in your industry?

If you're really good at something, don't do it for free.

- The Joker in The Dark Knight

Another great way to discover potential career or business opportunities is to take a look at your hobbies.

- What do you enjoy doing, even though you don't get paid for it?
- What do you do voluntarily?
- How do you spend your weekends?
- How do you want to spend your retirement?

I'm not that good at delayed gratification. I don't want to wait until after work to do what I love. I want to enjoy what I do every day. I want to do what I do best every day and get paid for it. If you are waiting for the end of the day, or the weekend, or retirement, to do

The Freak Factor

what you do best, take The Joker's advice. When you're really good at something, don't do it for free.

Despite the many benefits of doing your own thing, Jun Loayza, co-founder of Untemplater.com, cautions that entrepreneurship isn't for everyone. "The worst possible reason to become an entrepreneur is because you hate the corporate world. If you don't like your corporate job, it does not automatically follow that you will like starting your own company. It may just mean that you're in the wrong industry, the wrong company or that you chose the wrong career path.

Ask yourself, 'what career path suits me best?' You're going to have to figure this out on your own through trial and error and self reflection. If you've been an accountant for a year and you hate accounting, what are you still doing there? You should be networking, training yourself, and doing everything possible to change career paths into something you actually like to do."

Famous Freak: Peter Shankman

Peter Shankman is the founder of Help A Reporter Out, an email subscription service that connects journalists with experts that match the stories they're working on. In a recent blog post, he discussed how he has found the right fit for his weaknesses.

"Look, I talk all the time about how I have ADHD, how I use it to my advantage, blah, blah, blah, but let's seriously consider this for a second: What does that actually mean? I don't do well in offices, I don't do well in a structured environment, I sure as hell don't do well in a cubicle, and the last time I had a 'job' with a 'boss,' I quit within three months of starting.

I'm very fortunate to have realized it as early as I did, because what it tells me is that I'm simply not designed for working the way you work, but I've been smart enough to learn from it, and adapt my lifestyle to not only meet my needs, but exceed them, all while having fun."

Peter knows what he does well and what he doesn't do well. Most importantly, he knows where he fits and where he doesn't fit. Instead of trying to force himself into situations that don't match his unique style, he has created a distinctive way of working that is suited to him.

Freak Profile: Joseph Sherman

I first met Joseph when he attended my Freak Factor seminar at Duke University. We've talked many times since then and he's been a prolific commenter on my blog. His story is a great example of finding alignment.

"I venomously resisted the idea of not improving on my weaknesses. I thought the need to be well balanced was a universal law of business, just as gravity was a law of nature. Now I am learning to let go of my weakness so that I can focus on what I do well. I cannot be an exceptional international businessman ready to leave at a moment's notice to Morocco or Uzbekistan, and also be a dedicated cubicle staffer in an endless bureaucracy seeking the security of a government pension. For me, the cubicle must go. As I continue to let go, opportunities fitting my path have come easily to me. These opportunities have always been close to me, yet I did not see them because I was exhausted trying to make minute improvements on my weaknesses.

I have now left the cubicle for the freak show. I am working on projects that will let me be who I am while creating value for others. So many people try to fix themselves into being average so that they can have a safe job that will survive a recession. The current economic situation shows that the safe jobs are gone. I will be the most successful when I am myself, or perhaps when I let myself be the freak that is truly me."

Jon Mueller at 800-CEO-Read also recognized the importance of finding the right fit. "I can remember graduating college and not really knowing what to do, but knowing I needed 'a job.' So, jobs are what I got, and what a miserable few years it was. I wasn't thinking about how to get what I wanted, beyond the ability to pay bills. The tasks did not match my identity. Was I really contributing to those companies, to my community? I'm glad to say I realized early on that the answer to both those questions was 'no.' Today, I'm involved in work that fits who I am and it's great."

If we are overly joyful it's Friday, we should reconsider what
we're doing Monday through Thursday.

— Denise W. Barreto

Career Ideas for Freaks

Although many people have found jobs that allow them to flaunt their weaknesses, it is easy to conclude that there is no career that fits your unique flaws. But sometimes the perfect job for you is hiding inside the very words that you use to describe your shortcomings.

You have to be conceited to be a star.

- Simon Cowell, *American Idol*

Control Freaks

Maybe you are a **control** freak. I found a great blog post at *Business Pundit* offering ten jobs for control freaks. If you are a control freak, don't despair, just seek out one of these career opportunities.

1. Air Traffic Controller - "If they're not a control freak, people may die."

2. Military Officer

3. Chef

4. Surgeon - Another example of how being a control freak saves lives.

5. Business Consultant

6. Pilot

7. Professional Organizer - "A priceless manifestation of control-freakish tendencies."

8. CEO

9. Accountant - That's why the job title is "controller."

10. Architect

Maybe we should add movie director to the list. McG was the director for Terminator Salvation, Charlie's Angels and a variety of television and internet hits. In a recent Fast Company article he admitted to being a control freak. I love the interviewer's response to McG's confession. "As afflictions go, it would be hard to find one better suited for a media mogul - or any mogul for that matter - than a seemingly endless capacity for control. To call McG a control freak might be uncharitable. Let's just say he's extremely attentive to detail."

He goes on to describe the frenzy of activity and decision overload that characterize a movie set. This situation might overwhelm other people but, since McG is a control freak, this world is his "paradise." In other words, McG is a phenomenally successful and wealthy media mogul because of his weakness, not in spite of it. He has accomplished this by finding the perfect fit for his particular problem, a situation in which his apparent weakness is a powerful strength.

What's McG's next move? He's trying to find a way to gain even more control over the movie-making process by eliminating the studios from the process. He's flaunting his weakness by becoming even more of a control freak.

Critics

Maybe you're too critical. There are many jobs for that, including: food critic, music critic and movie critic. You could also look into becoming a judge.

Simon Cowell, the notorious judge on *American Idol*, is a big jerk. He is mean and unfair. He is critical and harsh. He is conceited and cruel. He makes fun of contestants' height, weight, attractiveness, clothing and singing ability or lack thereof. He is also fantastically successful. He makes more money for himself and his employer, Sony, than any other person in a similar position.

He is good, very good, maybe the best, at finding talented singers and helping them succeed in the music industry. He knows good singing, and bad singing, when he hears it. Despite the millions of people that despise him, he believes that he is honest and direct, not mean and nasty. He believes that he is actually doing people a favor when he confronts them with their lack of talent. He is trying to help them see the light and come to terms with their lack of ability so that they can move on with their lives.

In fact, he is critical of the parents, music teachers and friends who have failed to offer an honest assessment of many contestants' singing. Each of his strengths corresponds with one of his weaknesses. Is he honest or mean? Is he direct or harsh? Is he confident or conceited? He is all of these things and they are inseparable. Furthermore, whether you like him or not, he has found the perfect fit for his critical nature. They call it judging for a reason.

Analysts

If you're too analytical, become an analyst. Wikipedia lists more than 15 different types of analysts in a variety of fields and defines an analyst as an individual whose "primary function is a deep examination of a specific, limited area."

The whole secret of a successful life is to find out
what it is one's destiny to do, and then do it.

- Henry Ford

Even when the job isn't hiding inside the words themselves, your flaws still hold the clues to your ideal workplace.

Neat Freaks

If you're a neat freak, become a professional organizer. You'd probably be surprised by the number of specialties in this area, including: closet organizers, Feng Shui, ergonomics and space planning. You can get started by joining the National Association of Professional Organizers

Know-it-Alls

If you're a know-it-all, try teaching, fact-checking, researching or becoming an advice columnist.

FedEx Kinko's has a great commercial that highlights many common weaknesses. The main character goes around the room and asks each member of the team if they are going to continue to display the negative characteristics that they are known for. After each person confirms that they will continue their pattern of failure, he announces that he will go to FedEx Kinko's to get the help he needs to complete the project.

He does a great job diagnosing each person's weakness. However, it's easy to fall into the trap of thinking that these people are losers. They're not. Below I'll offer a few job ideas for each person along with a suggestion about the strength that matches their weakness.

Weakness	Strength	Ideal Jobs
Jeff keeps feeding him old information	He likes the past	Historian or museum curator
Dean is not living up to his resume	He's good at selling himself	Marketing, sales or public relations
Sue waffles and can't make a decision	She is flexible and open-minded	Politician or mediator
Jerome talks a big game but does nothing	He likes to talk	Talk show host or spokesperson
Rick folds under pressure	He likes peace and tranquility	Monk, yoga instructor or Zen gardener
Ted thinks everyone's out to get him	He is vigilant	Disaster planning or emergency management

A poor employee in one job can be superstar in another. How would it affect our behavior if we really believed this?

Famous Freak: Clay Marzo

Clay Marzo is the youngest surfer to ever score a perfect 10 in competition. He's so good that his fellow surfers describe him as "freaky," and they mean that as a compliment. Clay also has Asperger's syndrome, a form of autism that causes him to struggle in social situations.

After years of trying to discover what was wrong with him, Clay's mom gave up on having him tested for disorders and decided that "Clay is Clay." Unfortunately, other people weren't as accepting. When he wouldn't conform, people tried to make him fit in. One sponsor even dropped him because of his unusual behavior. Because he's different, Clay has been called "rude, lazy, dumb and shy." It is hard for people to see the positive side of his disability.

But, as an ESPN interview explained, he's "not a great surfer in spite of his medical condition, but rather, because of it." For example, people with Asperger's have a tremendous ability to focus on one thing, to the exclusion of everything else. This tunnel vision has helped Clay to excel in surfing. He might be uncomfortable interacting with people, but "in the water, there are no limits." He's found the right fit for his unique characteristics.

Avoidance is the next step to improving the alignment between who you are and what you do. You can't spend more time doing the right things until you stop doing the wrong things.

Reflect

Think of a time when you felt that you could just be yourself.

- Where were you?
- Who were you with?
- What were you doing?

Read

- Escape from Cubicle Nation by Pam Slim
- Career Renegade by Jonathan Fields
- Me 2.0 by Dan Schawbel
- Radical Careering by Sally Hogshead
- Free Agent Nation by Dan Pink
- The Brand You 50 by Tom Peters
- The Escape Artists by Joshua Piven

6. avoidance

move out of situations that highlight your weaknesses

You really can't try to do everything,
especially if you intend to be the best in the world.

- Seth Godin, *The Dip*

As I was boarding the plane recently, an attendant announced to all passengers that we were not allowed to open or eat any products containing peanuts on the flight and the airline would not be serving peanuts as a snack. Apparently, a passenger had a peanut allergy and they didn't want to take any chances. This seemed like an extreme approach but it's a good illustration of why avoidance works.

I think we are allergic to our weaknesses. Allergies and weaknesses are similar in a few ways. First, like allergies, we don't choose our weaknesses, they are natural. Second, you can't eliminate an allergy. Even medication just reduces the symptoms. There is no cure. Third, the obvious solution to an allergy, as we see in the plane illustration, is to avoid whatever you are allergic to. If it is peanuts, then stay away from peanuts. If disorganization is a weakness, avoid tasks that require you to be organized. If creativity is a weakness, avoid activities that require it.

Fourth, positive thinking has no effect on allergies. It doesn't matter if you wish you weren't allergic to peanuts or pretend that you're not. A peanut will still cause a horrible allergic reaction in your body. This is also true for weaknesses. No amount of wishful thinking will change the fact that you don't excel in this particular area. Don't sacrifice your happiness or success by continuing to attempt activities that involve your weaknesses. Treat them like bees, peanuts, dust or pollen. Avoid them at all costs.

Fifth, even if you are allergic to several things, there are millions of things that you aren't allergic to. Life will be far more enjoyable and productive if you spend your time and energy focused on the items that don't cause problems for you. Similarly, it is more effective to focus on areas of strength than to lament your areas of weakness.

As a child, I had severe hay fever that caused intense sneezing, severe congestion, runny nose and itchy eyes that left me debilitated for most of September each year. The solution was simple, air conditioning. It blocked the allergens and purified the air.

Don't put off until tomorrow what you can put off until the day after tomorrow and end up just as well.

— Mark Twain

Permanent Procrastination

The majority of my students and seminar participants believe that they have a problem with procrastination and many people cite this as their primary weakness. In fact, in most classes, every student admits to having a problem in this area. Books, articles, seminars and blog posts on overcoming procrastination are universally popular. Unfortunately, they don't work. People keep procrastinating. They can't help it. Why is it such a problem? Maybe it's not.

When I'm not doing something that comes deeply from me, I get bored. When I get bored I get distracted and when I get distracted, I become depressed. It's a natural resistance, and it ensures your integrity.

— Maria Irene Flores

Think of the activities that you really enjoy. These might include watching movies, golfing or shopping. Have you ever procrastinated these activities? Probably not. You don't procrastinate activities that you enjoy. You procrastinate activities that you don't enjoy and don't do well. Procrastination is an important clue that there is something you dislike about the activity you are avoiding and your distaste is a sure sign that you are dealing with an area of weakness. You wait to do these tasks until it is absolutely necessary because you'd rather be doing something else.

Procrastination isn't the problem, it's the solution.
So procrastinate now, don't put it off.

- Ellen DeGeneres

Procrastination is good. Procrastination is like a giant flashing sign saying, "This is not your thing." It is a sign that you have wandered away from your strengths, that you have strayed from those activities where you can have tremendous success. I don't want you to stop procrastinating. Instead of procrastinating less, I think you should actually procrastinate more. In fact, you should stop doing those activities altogether. I'd really like to see you procrastinate permanently.

Quitting is better than coping because
quitting frees you up to excel at something else.

- Seth Godin, *The Dip*

The cure for procrastination is to simply stop doing activities that you dislike. However, this certainly seems like an unrealistic suggestion and I'll spend the rest of the chapter providing support for this unconventional strategy.

Be Lazy

It's a cliché that "Necessity is the mother of invention." In other words, we invent things because we really need them. But I don't think that is true. We don't invent things because we need them. We invent things because we are lazy.

Necessity isn't the mother of invention. Laziness is the mother of invention. Think about it. Most inventions are "labor saving devices." They were developed by someone who was sick of doing something they didn't enjoy. Dishwashers allowed us to stop washing dishes. Washers and dryers let us stop washing and drying our own clothes. Vacuum cleaners saved us the trouble of cleaning our carpets. Bikes, motorcycles, cars, trains and planes take us where we want to go without any effort on our part. The desire to stop doing something can be a powerful force. Instead of resisting it, we should give in.

It is possible to do less and achieve more. As Keith Ferrazzi, author of Never Eat Alone, explains, "elegance is putting in the least amount of energy for the greatest return." Many people are suspicious of a work smarter not harder philosophy. However, the fact is that some activities simply have more value and will provide a greater return on your investment than others.

The Freak Factor

Eliminate blur. Stop multitasking. Stop allowing everything in.

- Chris Brogan

Stephen Covey, author of *The Seven Habits of Highly Effective People,* calls these high-leverage or "Quadrant 2" activities. They are important but they aren't urgent, so they often go undone. Here are a few activities that have a guaranteed payoff:

- Exercising
- Building relationships
- Planning
- Learning
- Sleeping

We've got the opportunity to do some really big things by just working on a few things, and by chalking up some little victories.

- Chris Brogan

The Pareto Principle, also known as the 80/20 rule, can be applied to a variety of situations. For example, at most companies, 80% of the profits come from 20% of the customers. Nonprofits get 80% of their donations from 20% of their donors. As it relates to personal productivity, it means that 80% of our results come from 20% of our efforts. This also means that the other 20% of our accomplishments come from 80% of our effort.

Quit or be exceptional. Average is for losers.

- Seth Godin, *The Dip*

In other words, some of our activities are more valuable than others. They aren't all equal. I believe that the majority of your results are coming from the time that you spend in your areas of strength and you are wasting the rest of your time and getting nowhere when you work in your areas of weakness. In order to improve our effectiveness, we need to eliminate activities that take a lot of time and effort but offer a small return.

To fulfill some commitments, others must be excluded.

- Chris Guillebeau, *The Art of Non-Conformity*

The advice to simply stop doing things you don't like might sound unreasonable, but that is because it is unconventional. Marcus Buckingham, author of *The One Thing You Need to Know*, argues that the most important thing to know about personal success is, "if you don't like it, stop doing it." Management guru Peter Drucker, calls this "organized abandonment," and Chris Guillebeau, author of *The Art of Non-Conformity*, refers to it as "radical exclusion." Tom Peters recommends that you go a step further and get a "stop counselor" to help you eliminate unnecessary or distracting tasks.

Wine guru and speaker, Gary Vaynerchuk, exhorts his audiences to "stop doing what you hate!" If you want more time, he also has another suggestion. "Stop watching f*ing episodes of Lost! Despite feeling like there is no extra time in the day, many people waste time on pursuits like cheesy television shows and meaningless Twitter conversations… Be ruthless with your time." Are you ruthless with your time?

A couple years ago I saw Jim Collins, author of *Good to Great*, speak at the Catalyst Conference in Atlanta. One of his primary suggestions was to create a stop-doing list. Good people and good companies have to-do lists, but the best also have lists of what they will stop-doing. Good activities distract us from what is best. We need to systematically eliminate these things from our lives.

We fail when we get distracted by activities
we don't have the guts to quit.

- Seth Godin, *The Dip*

He argued that the time we have is finite but the number of choices we have is infinite. Therefore, it is vital to choose precisely how to make the most of the limited time that we have. Below are a few suggestions, from Collins' website, for how to get started with your stop-doing list.

- Start an actual, physical list of things to stop doing.
- Every time you add a new activity to your to-do list, select an activity to stop doing.
- Rank each of your activities from most important to least important. Drop the bottom 20%.
- Blank page test: If this wasn't already on your list, would you add it now? If not, drop it.

The Freak Factor

- Don't devote financial, psychological or emotional resources to activities that don't pass the preceding tests.

Do more by doing less. Do more important stuff by eliminating less important stuff. Make tough decisions. What we don't do is just as important as what we do. I've tried this before and it works. Here are some things on my stop-doing list.

- Stop watching TV.
- Stop accepting fantasy football and NCAA tournament bracket invitations.
- Stop checking my online book sales rankings so often.
- Stop serving on boards that I'm not passionate about.
- Stop socializing with negative people who constantly complain.

Pruning

As a transplant to the South, I am enjoying the many new types of foliage. After several years, I am still amazed to see flowers bloom on bushes in early January. One very popular southern tree is the Crepe Myrtle. It caught my attention because of the way it is pruned. In the winter, you can see rows and rows of trees that have been cut back severely, with only the largest branches remaining. This annual pruning maintains the health and appearance of the tree.

Truly successful people, those who enjoy every part of their life and have financial stability, are very picky about where they spend their time and energy. So prune relentlessly.

- Pam Slim

I think it is the same for our lives. In our efforts to be well-rounded and multi-faceted, we often develop branches that are unproductive. Unfortunately, we don't prune them and they end up sapping our strength. Take a look at the branches in your life and then answer the following questions:

- Which branches are dead or dying?
- How much time and energy does it take to maintain those branches?
- What will it take to prune them?
- What are the consequences of not pruning them?
- Which branches are alive and fruitful?

- How can you focus more time and attention on them?
- How much more fruitful could they be if you removed the dead branches?

We all have a limited amount of time, energy and resources. Seasonal pruning keeps us from wasting those precious resources and, instead, allows us to focus on the areas with the most potential.

Saying No

In my blog I talk a lot about how successful people ruthlessly eliminate tasks that don't fit with their strengths. In my strategy classes I talk a lot about the importance of alignment between a company's vision, values and actions. I argue that what we choose to do is just as important as what we choose not to do. I tell everyone that sometimes, in trying to please one individual or group, we'll end up offending another individual or group.

I stand by those statements. However, I recognize that sometimes this is easier said than done. I've been doing speaking and training for almost ten years. In that time, I've never encountered a situation where I felt uncomfortable with an organization's mission. I've never had to say no. I've never felt the need to.

That changed recently. We were to the scheduling phase of a presentation when I decided to review the potential client's website. I didn't like what I found. I don't support what they do. In fact, I'm opposed to it. Their values clash with my values.

The easy choice would be to do the talk, collect the fee and rationalize that I'm just doing a presentation, that I'm not necessarily supporting their mission. The difficult choice would be to say no, to acknowledge that this presentation is not in alignment with my mission and values, that this isn't for me.

It wasn't easy to say no and it wasn't comfortable. I still have a bad feeling in my stomach. But I think this was the right choice. I chose to do what I thought was right. In doing so, I also chose to make some people unhappy. Saying yes to anything means saying no to something else. What will you say no to? Who will you say no to?

If quitters never win, and winners never quit, why do they say,
"Quit while you're ahead"?

- Timothy Cusack, *Twitter.com/TCusack247*

Be a Quitter

If at first you don't succeed, try try again. Stick with it. Persevere. Don't give up. This seems like good advice. It encourages self-discipline, effort and hard work. It is similar to the No Pain, No Gain perspective that is held by people who want you to get out of your comfort zone. But maybe it isn't always the best approach. Maybe you should quit and get back into your comfort zone.

Chris Bernheisel was the first contestant to audition for American Idol in Omaha, Nebraska. He was definitely a huge fan of the show. However, despite offering gifts to the judges, he was rejected. His singing was terrible.

Then something interesting happened. He asked if he could audition for something different. He wanted the opportunity to be a television reporter covering the show. His second audition was successful and he was told to come to Hollywood as a reporter for the local affiliate FOX 42.

This is a great lesson. Sometimes we shouldn't try again. We shouldn't persevere. Instead, we should audition for a different part. We should quit and move on to something that offers a better fit for our unique talents.

Are you sticking with it when you should be quitting? Is there a different part that you might be more qualified for? Could you audition for something else? Maybe you could end up in Hollywood with Chris.

Seth Godin has written a good book on this subject. It's called *The Dip: A Little Book that Teaches You When to Quit and When to Stick*. You can also read the free manifesto for The Dip at ChangeThis.com.

But if you stop doing all the things that you don't like to do, how will they get done? That's a good question and the answer is in the next chapter on affiliation.

Reflect

- Make a list of the activities that you commonly procrastinate.
- What is it about these activities that you don't enjoy?
- Refer to your list of weaknesses to identify potential similarities.
- List the activities that you do while you are procrastinating.
- While you are avoiding certain tasks, what do you do instead?
- What is it about these activities that you enjoy?
- Refer to your list of strengths to identify potential similarities.
- Does this task need to be completed?
- What would happen if you just stopped?
- If it has to be done, what are some alternative ways of ensuring that it is completed?
- Review your list of weaknesses.
- Reflect on a time when you were required to work in an area of weakness.
- How did it feel?
- What were the results?
- What activities are you currently engaged in that require you to overcome your weaknesses?
- What percentage of your time do you currently spend in your areas of weakness?
- How could you decrease that percentage?

Act

- Create a not-to-do list.
- List some worthwhile activities that you don't enjoy.
- Make a commitment to stop doing just one of those activities.

Read

- The Dip by Seth Godin
- First things First by Stephen Covey
- Good to Great by Jim Collins

7. affiliation

find people who are strong where you are weak

I get by with a little help from my friends.

- The Beatles

If you stop doing the things you don't like to do, as I suggested in the last chapter, how will they get done? One option is to form relationships with people who have strengths that complement your weaknesses. You don't need to be well-rounded but you can still live a balanced life by finding the right people to help you. Many people cite complementary partnerships as an essential component of their success. Microsoft's Bill Gates and Steve Ballmer are one example of this phenomenon.

However, close partnerships aren't the only way to minimize the impact of your weaknesses. Just like companies outsource aspects of their operations, you can also hire others to do tasks you don't like or don't do well. In doing so, you'll have more time and more energy for the work that you do best.

Don't Do it Yourself

Based on the popularity of the Do-It-Yourself (DIY) Network, it seems that Americans love to do it themselves. Every weekend people overcome the temptation to hire qualified and experienced trades people to complete plumbing, electrical and carpentry projects, choosing instead to do it themselves. It is an understandable impulse. It costs a lot to pay someone else to do the work. It is much cheaper to just do it yourself. Or so it seems.

I believe that it only seems cheaper to do it ourselves because we don't really calculate the cost. We calculate the cost of the materials but not the cost of our time. We also fail to count the cost of the opportunities that we miss while we are studying the subtleties of begonia fertilizer.

Economists refer to this as opportunity cost, which means that some activities are mutually exclusive. You want to do two things but you can't do them both. Pam Slim calls this displacement, which means that "everything that you do rules out something else that you can't do." Choosing one activity eliminates the possibility of doing the other activity. The opportunity cost is the price that you pay for missing out on the other option. This cost can be time, energy, money or anything else that you value.

If you've ever paid an ATM fee for withdrawing your money from another bank, you understand opportunity cost. You could have driven across town to your bank and withdrawn the money without paying a fee, but you decided that you'd rather spend the money on the fee than spend the time driving. You sacrificed your money, in order to save time.

There are other issues to consider as well. Is it really cheaper to do it yourself if you include your hourly rate in the cost? Although you might earn less per hour than the plumber, it will surely take you longer to complete the same task. It will also require you to buy tools or equipment that you will probably never use again.

Consider lawn care. How much does it really cost to mow your own lawn? You have to take into consideration the cost of the mower, weed-eater, edger, spreader, blower, gas, oil, repairs, etc. If you have a riding mower, the initial investment is huge. What if you would have invested that money into a good mutual fund? The earnings alone might have been enough to pay someone to cut your grass. Additionally, when working on projects that are more complex than lawn care, a competent plumber, electrician or carpenter can probably do it better than the weekend amateur. What will it cost if you do it wrong?

I think it is even more important to think about what you could be doing instead of doing-it-yourself. Instead of learning a little bit about something that you'll never do again, you could be increasing your expertise in a more relevant arena. You could earn more if you got more education or earned additional certifications. You could read a good book about your industry or profession. What is the long-term financial cost of missing out on all these opportunities, while you are learning to install replacement windows?

Instead of making friends with the clerk at the hardware store, you could be building relationship with your children or spouse. What are those relationships worth? It will certainly cost you more in the future if you don't build and maintain those relationships now.

Similarly, time spent trying to fix your weaknesses or forcing yourself to fit in takes away from time you could have spent building on your strengths or finding the right fit. We want to do it all but we can't.

Outsourcing

Pam Slim is "a big fan of outsourcing anything in your life that is not a core strength or a joy to do. As long as you focus your freed-up time to generate more revenue or opportunities, it is a good trade." We already outsource many life activities because we recognize that it isn't worth our time to complete them or because they can be done better by someone else. Throughout history, these tasks consumed almost every second of every day for most people.

- Growing food
- Harvesting food
- Cooking food
- Making fabric
- Sewing clothes
- Building houses
- Manufacturing vehicles

These may seem like obvious examples but they illustrate the wisdom of this approach. We just haven't taken it far enough. We have many more opportunities to stop doing it ourselves than we take advantage of.

- Stop shopping, even for groceries - Use Amazon Grocery or Peapod or My Girlfriend's Kitchen
- Stop changing your oil or doing any vehicle maintenance - Go to Jiffy Lube
- Stop washing your car - Take it to a car wash
- Stop cleaning your house - Hire Merry Maids
- Stop doing your taxes - Find a good accountant or use HR Block
- Stop managing your own investments - Find a local independent advisor
- Stop mowing your grass - Pay a neighborhood kid to do it or make your kids do it

Now, add up how much time you would save each week if you stopped doing these activities. Then, start a new list. What could you do instead? How could you invest your time and energy so that it will pay off over the long-term? Here are some ideas.

- Start your own business
- Go back to school
- Spend more time with your kids
- Attend a seminar
- Start a blog
- Read a good book
- Start exercising
- Write a book
- Volunteer

Some of these suggestions might seem small but I know from personal experience that eliminating low-leverage tasks to make room for high-leverage activities can create big breakthroughs. I hate any kind of routine maintenance activities and mowing the lawn is one of the worst. As soon as I'm done cutting the grass, it just starts growing right back. My wife would always complain because I waited too long and let the grass get too tall. Our new yard in North Carolina is huge and it took almost three hours each week to take care of it. During the middle of the summer it was even worse. It needed to be mowed every five days, instead of once a week.

I had a decision to make. I wanted my wife to have a nice yard but I also wanted to spend time with my wife and kids and start my own business. I couldn't do it all. I didn't have enough time.

So I decided to hire the neighbor's son to mow the grass. I paid him $20, which was about $7 per hour. Then I took the three hours that I was spending on the lawn and dedicated it to my business. I purchased a website address and hired my friend to create a website. My father-in-law, who is a graphic designer, helped me create business cards. I started going to events at the local Chamber of Commerce and began work on my first book. It wasn't much, just three hours a week. But it was enough to create momentum and allow me to still do the other things that were really important to me.

It's been seven years since I started my business and each year has been more successful than the last. I've certainly made more than enough money to pay someone to handle our landscaping needs. But I never would have had any of this success if I was still mowing my own grass.

I'd encourage you to start by outsourcing the tasks that you dislike the most. They probably aren't a good fit for you and they cost you time, energy and stress. Once you pay to save yourself some time, invest the time in an activity that you are good at and that you enjoy. You'll be rewarded with additional energy, fulfillment and confidence, which will lead to more money in the future, either directly or indirectly.

One objection that I usually get to outsourcing is that people can't afford it. This is a chicken or the egg argument. My point is that the only way to improve your current financial situation is to stop doing those things that distract you from doing what you do best. If you can't afford it now, the only way you'll ever be able to afford it is to actually do it. It will pay off in the long run.

I know this is true because I've done it. I have to admit, I am a recovering Do-It-Yourselfer. I used to do everything by myself until I realized what it was actually costing me. I grew up poor. I started delivering papers at 5am each day when I was 12 so that I didn't have to go to school with patches in my pants. When I graduated from college, I had seven different jobs. I never paid someone to do something that I could do myself. I didn't even eat out very much because it was cheaper to make my own meals. But there is a limit to how many jobs you can have and how many hours you can work. Hard work is important but it has its limits.

Education was one way that I improved my situation. But this required that I work less in order to focus on my studies. I also had to pay for my classes. This trade-off didn't make sense in the short-term. It was a long-term investment. Outsourcing is also a long-term

The Freak Factor

investment. Hiring someone to cut my grass was the best investment I ever made. I now make enough money giving a one-hour presentation to pay for two years of lawn care.

Now that I'm self-employed, I'm a free agent. I don't have any employees and I'm not planning to hire any. But there are a lot of skills that I don't have and don't want to learn. I want to stay focused on the things that I do best, which basically include speaking and writing. In order to do this, I outsource almost every aspect of my business. Eric Smoldt at Group 3 does all of my graphic design. He designed the cover and formatted this book. Michelle Verhaeghe helps me with website design. Peggy King at Parker & Parker handles my accounting and taxes. The leading online bookseller handles the processing and shipping for all of my products. CreateSpace prints my books, CDs and DVDs on demand when they are ordered by a customer. There is no inventory. Dan "Jiffy" Jones changes the oil in my cars on the road in front of my house. I don't even have to leave home.

Before we had our third daughter, my wife decided that she wanted to get a graduate degree in management. This meant that we'd need to take out $30,000 in student loans. I didn't hesitate because it seemed like a good investment. But it would take more than money for her to graduate. It would take time and I didn't have any. I was teaching full-time at one school, part-time at two graduate schools and building my business. In my spare time I took care of our daughters so that Stephanie could study and write papers.

One night I was working on my laptop in the living room at 11:00pm and noticed my wife moving the chairs out of the kitchen so that she could sweep and mop the floor. My first instinct was to tell her not to worry about it, but I knew that wouldn't work. She likes things to be clean. I wanted to help but I hate to clean and didn't have the time.

We had a choice to make. Was I going to sacrifice high-leverage activities, like building my business, and high-value activities, like spending time with my children, to become a maid? Or was Stephanie going to stop going to school in order to keep the house in order? Neither of these choices was acceptable.

So I did a quick calculation. With her master's degree, my wife could teach college courses on a part-time basis and earn at least $1500 per class. It would cost $120 per month to hire someone to clean the house every two week. This meant that Stephanie could pay for almost an year of cleaning by teaching just one course. We hired a cleaning lady and never looked back.

One primary advantage of being a nudist
is that you don't have to do laundry.

- Quote from my wife after folding clothes for an hour.

Now, I am trying to eliminate every conceivable activity. Laundry takes up a lot of time but taking all the clothes to the cleaners doesn't seem feasible and I'm not ready to become a nudist. I'm currently looking for other options.

You'd probably be surprised by what can be outsourced. For a very humorous discussion of outsourcing personal and business tasks, read AJ Jacobs' article, *My Outsourced Life*. He outsourced his worries to an assistant in India and even asked his virtual assistant to apologize to his wife for him.

Outsourcing is just one way to take care of things that you don't like. You can also partner with family members, friends, co-workers and people in your community. But there are two barriers to doing this. First, we believe that no one wants to do the tasks that we dislike. Second, we want other people to accept our weaknesses, but we don't want to accept their flaws.

Dirty Jobs

One of the problems with finding people to do tasks we find is that we believe that the task itself is inherently disagreeable. We tell ourselves that nobody wants to do it. Nobody likes it. But that's not true. There is always someone who loves to do what you hate to do. They love the task for the same reason that you hate it. For example, you hate repetition. It bores you. But there is someone else that loves the routine and certainty of repetitive tasks. It soothes them.

Dirty Jobs, the popular TV show starring Mike Rowe, profiles people involved in all sorts of objectionable tasks like cleaning portable toilets, raising turkeys, treating sewage, repairing giant tires or making bricks. But the show proves the adage that "One man's trash is another man's treasure." Although these jobs seem disgusting, the people who do them usually seem to be enjoying themselves. There is something about the job that they like. Maybe they want to be outside or work with their hands or be alone or see the finished product.

My friend, Tom Morris, speaker and author of *If Aristotle Ran General Motors*, told me about a woman in his city that has her own business cleaning up dog poop from people's back yards. At first blush, this doesn't seem like a very good business idea. However, you have to remember that she quit her job and chose to start this kind of business. Why would she do that? There are three reasons. First, she likes to work independently. It doesn't matter what she's doing. She'd rather be her own boss than work for someone

The Freak Factor

else. Second, she likes to be active. Her job allows her to move, instead of being stuck in a chair all day. Third, she likes to be outside. Since dogs usually poop outside, this is a perfect fit.

Symbiosis

Symbiosis is defined by Wikipedia as "an interaction between two organisms living together in intimate association or the merging of two dissimilar organisms." A better definition is a mutually beneficial relationship between organisms with differing abilities and needs. In other words, a symbiotic relationship is one in which two parties help each other by providing something that the other party needs but can't provide for themselves.

For example, the Nile crocodile can't floss its teeth. Its arms aren't long enough and it doesn't have any floss. The Egyptian Plover, a bird, helps the crocodile by walking around in its mouth and picking food and other debris out of the crocodile's teeth. The crocodile could easily crush the bird and swallow it whole. But it doesn't because the bird provides a needed service. The plover gets a free meal, and the protection of a fearsome predator, and the crocodile gets free dental care. It is a win-win situation.

We can create similar symbiotic relationships in our life and work, although I still can't find anyone who wants to floss my teeth. Graham Shevlin, an IT consultant and blogger at GrahamShevlin.com, explains how our weaknesses can be offset by the right partner. "Ever since I can remember, I have been a night owl. This often gives me challenges. Most corporations, especially in the USA, are set up around the 'morning lark' model. I have encountered the chill wind of disapproval from morning larks many times in the past when I roll into work and the larks have been working for 2-3 hours already. The fact that I am still working when they are flaked out on a couch somewhere is something that they seem to have a large capacity to ignore.

It is possible to form symbiotic working relationships with somebody who is opposite to you on the sleep and work spectrum. Many years ago in the UK, I had an extremely productive working relationship with a fellow project leader. She was a classic morning lark, she was in the office by 6am nearly every morning, but left by 4pm. By her own admission, her brain ceased to fire on all cylinders around 3pm.

We would meet together to work issues and set direction from 11am until 2pm, after which time I stayed away from her, since she would be winding down and not at her best. She would stay away from me until 11am, since before that time my brain was not firing on all cylinders. This worked well for our time together."

Graham's story reminded me of the old nursery rhyme about Jack Sprat.

Jack Sprat could eat no fat,

his wife could eat no lean.

And so between them both you see,

they licked the platter clean.

This is a good example of how partnerships at home can work effectively. My wife, Stephanie, is a great cook. She seems to have a natural gift for making food that tastes good, even if she doesn't have the exact ingredients that the recipe requires. She also enjoys the creative process of putting a complete meal together. I don't like to do any of that. If it was up to me, I'd just eat food that didn't require any preparation.

But we're a good team because Stephanie hates to clean up after a meal. She's so exhausted from making it, that she can't stand the thought of taking care of the mess. That is where I come in. I'm a finisher. I like to wrap things up. I like to get things done, especially when it is a small and manageable task.

However, it's easy to fail to appreciate this kind of partnership. I could complain that Stephanie never helps with the clean-up. She could complain that I never help with the cooking. Instead of accepting our unique roles and preferences, we could both spend our time complaining about what the other person doesn't do.

Imperfect People

We all want to be accepted for who we are. We want people to accept our quirks and limitations. Unfortunately, we are often unwilling to do this for others. The Freak Factor isn't just about you, your weaknesses and their corresponding strengths. It is also about the people around you, your co-workers, family and friends.

What bothers you most about the people in your life? Try to find the strength that corresponds with their most obvious weaknesses and then go one step further. Don't just tolerate their uniqueness, encourage them to flaunt it. If you do this, you will see a dramatic improvement in your relationships and people will probably respond differently to your freakness as well. Differentiation requires you to be unique and that often means accepting and encouraging imperfection in yourself and others.

For example, Tom Peters wrote an interesting blog post about the value of people who do the last two-percent. The people who make sure it is just right; the people who take care of the seemingly minor details; the people who ensure that everything is perfect before a presentation is made or a project is submitted. Full disclosure: I am not one of these people.

In the last few lines he says "sometimes we call the last two-percenter a 'pain in the ass.' True, but no one is of greater importance to the success of what we do." Are you a "two-percenter?" Are you a "pain in the ass?" If you aren't a two-percenter, consider the possibility that the pain caused by these people is a small price to pay for the value they deliver. If we want other people to accept our freak factor, we need to be willing to accept theirs as well.

Last year I downloaded the new Pearl Jam album, *Backspacer*, from iTunes and it included a short video about the band. The following quote from one of the band members caught my attention. "We sort of have our own thing and it's raw and it's an imperfect combination of personalities and we put a lot of faith in Ed (Eddie Vedder) as the artistic director to take bits and pieces from everybody and, in the end, he ties us together."

Sometimes we believe that success requires a perfect combination of personalities but the enduring success of Pearl Jam demonstrates that our imperfections can be combined to create something incredible. We need to acknowledge and accept people's imperfections and then tie them all together in a unique way. We need to stop looking for perfect people to partner with and start working with the imperfect people that we already know. We need to be the artistic directors of our own lives.

Affiliation isn't just about finding people who are strong where you are weak, it is also about finding people who like you just the way you are. It is about finding your community, finding your people, fellow freaks.

Choose Your Audience

"Know your audience." This is the conventional wisdom for speakers. If you know your audience, you can adapt the message to fit their particular needs. For example, giving a presentation to a kindergarten class is a lot different than giving a keynote speech to 500 managers. There is some truth to this but it assumes that you have the ability to make this adjustment.

Intellectually, I know that I can't talk to kindergartners the same way that I talk to adults, but that doesn't mean I have the skill to capture the attention of the five-year olds. Knowing your audience and being able to give them what they want are two different things.

Furthermore, there are some people who just aren't interested in what you have to say. No amount of effort will change that. I once did a presentation on how nonprofits start businesses that sold products and services to earn money to support their mission. One of the women in the audience worked for an anti-capitalistic (anti-business) activist organization. I'm not sure why she chose to attend but there was nothing that I could say that would fit with her perspective.

That is why, instead of knowing your audience, you should choose your audience. Instead of adapting your message to the audience, you should find the right audience for your message. You should find out who your ideal audience is and who is open to your message. Find out who is attracted to your approach and perspective and then communicate with those people.

> There's a message for every audience and
> an audience for every message.
>
> – Olalah Njenga

Larry the Cable Guy, a comedian on the Blue Collar Comedy Tour, is obnoxious, immature, gross and prejudiced. Many people find his act incredibly offensive. But when tickets go on sale for his show at a local sports arena, they usually sell out. In one night he earns $250,000, even though a lot of people have never heard of him and some of those who have don't like him.

Larry chooses his audience and they choose him. He doesn't try to convert people that don't like him and he doesn't try to adapt his style to make everyone happy. He seeks out people who enjoy his brand of comedy and gives them what they want.

Pam Slim believes that it is important for each of us to find "our people." "These are not just those people who would grudgingly fork over money for your product or service; they are people who would clamor to do business with you because you are the exact answer to their problems. They are your ideal partners, clients, customers, and mentors. These are people whom you like to spend time with, who embrace you despite your perceived warts, mistakes, and flaws and who are deeply affected by your work."

The right people will not reject you for being yourself, for being real. Don't try to please everyone. Try to please the right people.

The ability to choose who judges your work is the key building
block in becoming an artist in whatever you do.

- Seth Godin

Seth Godin narrows the definition of the right people to focus on those that tell others
about your company, product and/or service. You have to find these people and build
relationships with them. You can pay attention to the people who criticize your work or
you can identify those that appreciate your unique approach and develop deeper partnerships with them.

One way to partner with "your people" is through affiliate relationships. The internet has
made these very popular. It allows people who promote your products to earn a commis-
sion from the sale of those products. If you've developed a great product or service but
don't like marketing or sales, finding affiliates can be a great way to compensate for your
weakness.

Surprisingly, we can even create partnerships with our competition. Sharlyn Lauby, the
HR Bartender, explains that our competitors could actually be potential collaborators.
"I've discovered the best way to deal with competition is to point it inward. When I meet
people who really have it together and inspire me, instead of focusing my energies on
squashing them, I use that energy to make myself better. There are two reasons for doing
it. First, I get better at something. Second, I can eventually collaborate with that awesome person."

To succeed, you must delegate everything
except that which is your genius work.

- Fabienne Fredrickson

Freak Profile: Jennifer Schuchmann

Jennifer Schuchmann (pronounced shook-man), is a writer from Atlanta. In addition to writing, she leads workshops for aspiring writers. But she has two big weaknesses. First, she doesn't have a lot of original ideas, which makes it difficult to come up with something to write about. Second, she isn't good with spelling and grammar, a seemingly vital skill for a writer. So, how did her book, *First Things First*, end up on the New York Times bestseller list? I'll let Jennifer tell you in her own words.

"I have a very hard time coming up with ideas. I respond well to specifics, tell me you need a paragraph about how to make furniture from nuts and I can think of 80 things to say. Tell me to write about whatever I want and I can't think of a thing."

Because of this she thought, "I could never be a writer. Spelling and diagramming sentences just didn't interest me. I could look at the same sentence… and not see the mistakes. My brain just didn't focus on that. So in high school, I stopped writing. I realized I apparently didn't have what it takes to be a writer. I didn't have ideas and I didn't have the technical skills 'good writers' had."

But then she had an epiphany. "I was in a workshop listening to a publisher talk about how writers are in love with their own words. I thought to myself, 'I'm not.' From that moment I realized that I was different from the other writers I had met in the past. I realized that I was a writer who takes assignments. There are stories or articles that need to be told, and writers who are too passionate about their own ideas… can't write those stories, but I could.

Now less than ten years later, I've already published five books, all collaborations with other people. My latest book, *First Things First*, with Kurt and Brenda Warner was an assignment to write 75,000 words in 19 days. The book is now out and yesterday was number ten on the New York Times best seller list for hardcover nonfiction.

What has changed? Well, I've learned to embrace the fact that I can get behind other people's ideas, that not having my own isn't a hindrance to being a writer. And in the case of being a collaborative writer, not being married to my own ideas is a really good

The Freak Factor

thing. My agent continues to remind me that the ability to write fast is a unique skill. I've learned to compensate for misspellings or verbs that don't agree by hiring an outside editor or other writer who has those skills to look through my manuscript before I submit it.

 I teach at a lot of writers' conferences and I tell my story so that writers realize they need to capitalize on their strengths and find ways to compensate for their perceived weaknesses."

Jennifer's story demonstrates the power of affiliation. She proves that it is possible to have tremendous success without fixing your weaknesses. She has succeeded by embracing her flaws because she sees the strengths that are hiding inside them. For example, because she is not restricted by the traditional rules of spelling and grammar, she can write quickly. She deals with this apparent weakness easily by hiring people to edit her work.

Because she is not bursting with ideas of her own, she is open to the ideas of others. She capitalizes on this weakness by helping others to tell their stories. I experienced her gift for understanding during our phone conversation. She immediately understood the freak factor and sometimes explained the concept even better than I could.

Act

- Offer to help one of your friends or family members in their weak areas.
- I proofread stuff for my friend with dyslexia and he offers creative ideas for my audio and video resources.
- Who could you help?

Reflect

- Who are some of your best friends?
- Consider their strongest characteristics and compare them to your own.
- Who could you partner with that would offset your weaknesses?
- What tasks do you already outsource?
- What other activities do you rely on others to complete?
- Review your list of disliked tasks from the last chapter.
- Who could you hire to perform those tasks?
- How much time would you save?
- What would it cost?
- What could you do with the time that you saved?
- Could you earn enough during that time to defer the cost?
- If not, can you see how it could be worth it over the long-term?

Read

- The Four-Hour Work Week by Tim Ferriss

assessment

Please respond YES or NO to the following questions without reading your responses from the first chapter.

Once you've completed it, you can compare your results on both assessments.

_____ 1. It is important to fit in at work.

_____ 2. If I want to improve, I need to fix my weaknesses.

_____ 3. I try to build on my strengths, instead of trying to fix my weaknesses.

_____ 4. My job is a good fit for my personality, skills, and interests.

_____ 5. I accept other people's flaws and quirks.

_____ 6. It is important to be well-rounded, especially at work.

_____ 7. I should spend time fixing my weaknesses and building my strengths.

_____ 8. I avoid activities that don't fit my personality, skills, and interests.

_____ 9. Having a well-balanced set of characteristics will make me more marketable.

_____ 10. Being different and sticking out will help me to be more successful in my career.

_____ **Total**

scoring key

1 point each for answering YES to questions 3, 4, 5, 8, 10
1 point each for answering NO to questions 1, 2, 6, 7, 9

Future Freak *(1-2 points)*

You definitely have the potential to become a freak. It seems like you are stuck in situations that don't value your unique characteristics and you're spending a lot of time trying to fix your weaknesses.

Temporary Freak *(3-4 points)*

You're on your way to becoming a freak. It seems like you sometimes build on your strengths but also believe that it is important to fix your weaknesses. You feel like it is important to fit in and be well-rounded at work.

Part-time Freak *(5-6 points)*

You're moving up on the freakness scale. It seems like you're starting to look for situations that make your weaknesses irrelevant and you've begun to see that fixing your weaknesses is an ineffective strategy.

Certified Freak *(7-8 points)*

You are near the top of the freakness scale. You're flaunting your weaknesses most of the time. You avoid most activities that highlight your weaknesses and seek out situations that maximize your strengths.

Superfreak *(9-10 points)*

You are at the pinnacle of freakness. You flaunt your weaknesses and focus on your strengths. You're seeking out the right fit for your unique characteristics and partnering with people that have complementary skills. You also accept other people's freak factor and encourage them to freak out. As a superfreak, are you ready to help others maximize their freak factor?

* This assessment is also available online at freakfactorbook.com/quiz

online resources

take the freak factor **quiz**   freakfactorbook.com

listen to **interviews** and read the **blog**   www.daverendall.typepad.com

download the **free Freak Factor eBook**   freakfactorbook.com

download the **free Freak Factory eBook**   changethis.com/64.04.FreakFactory

watch my **video** clips on **YouTube**   youtube.com/drendall

follow me on **Twitter**   twitter.com/daverendall

join me on **Facebook**   facebook.com/daverendall

connect with me on **LinkedIn**   linkedin.com/in/daverendall

send me an **email**   dave@drendall.com

hire me to **speak** at your company or event   drendall.com

additional titles   By David Rendall

CREATE! Initiating Change and Inventing the Future

Individuals and businesses are constantly confronted with rapidly accelerating change. Effective leaders of the future will need to not only adapt to change but also create individual and organizational transformation. Unfortunately, most people and organizations resist change and are not aware of future trends. This session will explore methods for managing resistance to change as well as ways to become a creative person and an innovative leader.

Live Seminar DVD
Live Seminar CD

DEAD LEADERS Lessons from the Lives and Violent Deaths of the World's Most Influential People

Do you want to become a great leader? What does it take to achieve greatness? When I ask audiences to identify the greatest leaders in the history of the world, a few names always make the list. After asking this question repeatedly over the years, I finally noticed something. The leaders, who were consistently rated as great, shared one thing in common. They had all been killed. They didn't die natural deaths. They were either executed or assassinated. This led me to explore the lessons that we can learn from their example. During that journey, I discovered four leadership principles that have the power to transform your leadership and your legacy.

Live Seminar DVD
Live Seminar CD

EXPLORE! Understanding Ten Trends that are Changing the Future

Do you wish that you could predict the future? I can't give you the winning lottery numbers but I can share a simple strategy for accurately predicting what will happen next. Globalization, outsourcing, demographic shifts and technological advances are just a few of the seismic changes causing dramatic shifts in the way people live, work and play. These changes are combining and accelerating their impact on the world. This impact is both positive and negative, creating opportunities and threats, hope and fear. It is important for everyone to understand these trends and how they affect the future of their lives, careers and organizations.

Live Seminar DVD
Live Seminar CD

FOCUS! Organizing Your Time and Leading Your Life

Are you too busy? Do you feel overwhelmed? Are you constantly being pulled in too many different directions? Is it hard to find time for the things that really matter? Time management is more than just checking items off a to-do list or squeezing a few more minutes out of each day by multi-tasking. In fact, these activities can often be counterproductive. In order to increase effectiveness and restore your peace of mind, it is essential to clarify purpose, develop plans, prioritize activities, and proactively execute those priorities each day. This seminar will show you how to:

- Develop a clear direction for your life
- Set and achieve meaningful goals
- Focus energy on high priority activities
- Align daily tasks with long-term objectives
- Manage interruptions effectively

Live Seminar DVD
Live Seminar CD

THE FREAK FACTOR: Discovering Uniqueness by Flaunting Weakness

Let me ask you a question. What's your problem? I'm serious. What do you wish you could change about yourself? What is the complaint that you hear the most from those closest to you, your friends, co-workers, and family members? Are you too loud or too quiet, too hyperactive or too sedentary, too organized or too messy? You get the idea.

So, what should you do? Most people think that they should find and fix their weaknesses. Unfortunately, this just leads to frustration and failure. Your weaknesses are actually the best clue to your strengths. Furthermore, building your strengths, not fixing your weaknesses, is your best strategy for success.

This seminar is designed to encourage you to become more of who you are, not to turn you into someone else. It's about becoming more different and more unique, not more average and more mediocre. You will learn how to:

- Discover your distinctive strengths and weaknesses
- Frame your unique characteristics in a positive way
- Find situations that highlight your positive qualities
- Maximize your self-control
- Implement permanent procrastination
- Flaunt your weaknesses

Live Seminar DVD
Live Seminar CD

THE FREAK FACTORY Making Employees Better by Helping Them Get Worse

Are you frustrated by disengaged and unproductive employees? Are you looking for better strategies for improving employee performance?

Research shows that most people are not committed to their jobs and the way we currently manage employees does even more to harm, instead of help, their performance. We think our employees are broken, treat them like they are broken, and then wonder why they don't work. Instead of attacking people's weaknesses, we need to find the strength that is hidden inside their apparently negative characteristics.

It is time to stop trying to create well-rounded and balanced employees. We need people that are unbalanced. We need freaks. This session will explore eight essential strategies for improving employee engagement by turning our teams, departments or organizations into freak factories.

Live Seminar DVD
Live Seminar CD

GROW! Ten Strategies for Maximizing Your Leadership Potential

Do you want to increase your influence? Are you looking for practical ways to improve your leadership? Effective leaders recognize the importance of continuous learning and personal development. They are also dedicated to empowering and training others. Based on the fourth factor of effective leadership, improvement, this seminar offers ten proven methods for leadership development, including strategies for personal growth and developing other leaders.

Live Seminar DVD
Live Seminar CD

LEAD! The Four Factors of Effective Leadership

This resource combines the wisdom of ancient philosophers, successful executives and leadership gurus into a clear roadmap for effective leadership. The four factors focus on common themes that can be found throughout most advice on leadership and interpersonal effectiveness. These factors demonstrate that:

- Everyone can be a leader
- Leadership begins with you
- Leadership is a relationship
- Leadership produces positive change

Hardcover Book
Paperback Book
Audiobook (Unabridged)
Live Seminar DVD
Live Seminar CD

PERSUADE! Nine Strategies for Getting What You Want

Do you always get what you want? Why do some attempts succeed while others fail? What can you do to improve your ability to convince others? Whether you work in sales, fund development or organizational management, powerful persuasion is an essential element of your success. This seminar will explore nine fundamental principles of human behavior and help you harness that knowledge to persuade the people around you. You will learn how to:

- Influence people's thoughts, feelings and behaviors
- Establish and maintain credibility
- Find the right audience
- Make big changes by starting small
- Create vivid appeals

Live Seminar DVD
Live Seminar CD

RECHARGE! Managing Stress and Avoiding Burnout

Are you burned out? Do you feel overwhelmed by personal and professional stress? If you want to recharge yourself and reclaim control of your physical, emotional and mental well-being, this seminar can help. We will explore the causes and symptoms of burnout, as well as six proven stress management strategies. You will learn how to:

- Take control of your responses to stress
- Focus on what is really important
- Use passion to overcome pain
- Develop a new perspective on stress
- Build relationships to prevent burnout
- Balance activity and renewal

Live Seminar DVD
Live Seminar CD

Purchase any of these titles at **www.drendall.com/david_rendall_resources.html**

notes:

notes:

Made in the USA
Charleston, SC
13 March 2011